A Stylometric Study
of the
NEW TESTAMENT

ANTHONY KENNY

CLARENDON PRESS · OXFORD
1986

Oxford University Press, Walton Street, Oxford OX2 6DP
Oxford New York Toronto
Delhi Bombay Calcutta Madras Karachi
Kuala Lumpur Singapore Hong Kong Tokyo
Nairobi Dar es Salaam Cape Town
Melbourne Auckland
and associated companies in
Beirut Berlin Ibadan Nicosia

Oxford is a trade mark of Oxford University Press

Published in the United States
by Oxford University Press, New York

British Library Cataloguing in Publication Data
Kenny, Anthony
A stylometric study of the New Testament.
1. Bible. N.T.—Authorship
I. Title
225.6'6 BS2325
ISBN 0-19-826178-0

Library of Congress Cataloging in Publication Data
Kenny, Anthony John Patrick.
A stylometric study of the New Testament.
Bibliography: p.
Includes index.
1. Bible. N.T.—Language, style. I. Title.
BS2385.K393 1986 225.4'8 86-8436
ISBN 0-19-826178-0

Typeset by Joshua Associates Limited
Printed in Great Britain
at the University Printing House, Oxford
by David Stanford
Printer to the University

Preface

THE present book began as the Speaker's Lectures on Biblical Studies in the University of Oxford in the years 1979-81. My stylometric work on the New Testament, presented in those lectures, was transformed when I learnt of the machine-readable parsed New Testament prepared by Barbara and Timothy Friberg at the Computer Center of the University of Minnesota. I am indebted to Professor Patten and the staff of that Center for their kindness to me during a sabbatical in Minneapolis in 1981, and for the gift of microfiches of a concordance based on the Fribergs' text. I am also indebted to the staff of the Oxford Computer Service for friendly help over the years, in particular to Susan Hockey, Catherine Griffin, and Paul Griffith, and to those at the Oxford University Press who have been involved in the editing and production of the book, especially Angela Blackburn and John Waś. I am most grateful to the Rev. Michael Humphreys, who read through the typescript and saved me from a number of errors.

I have been critical of some of the methods and conclusions of A. Q. Morton. But I would like to pay tribute to the pioneering work he has done in stylometry, and the vigour with which, in his published writings, he has communicated the excitement of stylometric study.

A. K.

Balliol College
October 1983

Contents

List of Figures

List of Tables

Note on Sources

WHERE the source is given as Davison or Morgenthaler, the tables are reproduced or extracted from the published works mentioned in the bibliography.

Where the source is given as Aland, the table is compiled from the 'Wortstatistik' in volume II of the *Vollständige Konkordanz*. Where necessary, this has been corrected in the light of F. Neirynck's article cited in the bibliography.

Where the source is given as Fribergs, the table is based on hand-counts made by myself from the microfiche concordance to the machine-readable version of the *Analytical Greek New Testament*. Statistical calculations were performed on these word-counts either on a Texas Instruments programmable 58 calculator or with the SPSS package on the ICL 2988 machine in the Oxford University Computing Service.

I

Introduction

WHAT is stylometry? Stylometry is the study of quantifiable features of style of a written or spoken text. Such a study may be undertaken for several different reasons. One may wish to study the statistics of word usage or word order with a view to understanding a text better, to catch nuances of meaning and perhaps to render them into a different language. Or one may be interested in the history of the development of a language, and study the speech habits of particular authors as an indication of linguistic change. Or one may hope to use the quantifiable features of a text as an indication of the authorship of a text when this is in question. It is in this context of problems of authorship attribution that the present contribution to the stylometry of the New Testament is offered.

The use of stylometry in authorship attribution studies depends on the hypothesis that there are quantifiable features of style which are characteristic of particular authors. Ideally, a stylometric test of authorship should be a feature which is characteristic of all the known works of a particular author and which is unique to his works. Features which are to be found in all, and only, the works of a particular author are often not easy to come by. Authorship attribution problems are easier to deal with when they can be cast into the following form: in respect of the measured features, does the doubtful work resemble the work of candidate author A more than it resembles the work of candidate author B? Problems of disputed authorship in the New Testament, unfortunately, do not present themselves in this simple pattern. But it is possible to see which parts of the New Testament resemble other parts more or less closely, and on the basis of this to make reasonable conjectures about authorship.

An early proposal for the stylometric study of the New Testament was made in 1851 when Augustus de Morgan suggested that disputes about the authenticity of some of the writings attributed to

St Paul might be settled by ascertaining the mean length, in letters, of the words used in the various Epistles. More recently it is sentence-length, rather than word-length, which has been offered as a criterion of authorship to resolve the Pauline problem. W. C. Wake, and after him A. Q. Morton, studied the length of sentences in the Epistles, and made extensive comparisons with sentence-lengths in other Greek authors. They concluded that the variability in sentence-lengths between Epistles was beyond parallel in any of the other authors studied. On the basis of this, and of the occurrences of a number of frequent conjunctions and particles, Morton in *Paul, the Man and the Myth* (1966) concluded that Romans, 1 and 2 Corinthians, and Galatians formed a homo-geneous group which could be attributed to the Apostle Paul; between this group and the other Epistles there were a large number of significant differences, some of them larger than any differences known to exist in the writings of any other Greek author, regardless of literary form or variation over time. The other Epistles, Morton suggested, might come from as many as six different hands. Morton has returned to the topic in a number of subsequent studies, offering fresh evidence from different stylistic features, all, he claims, pointing towards the same conclusion. A striking feature of Morton's work is that it reached, by quite different methods, conclusions first suggested by F. C. Baur at Tübingen in the early nineteenth century.

Other stylometric studies have concentrated on vocabulary fre-quency. Long before the invention of computers and the develop-ment of statistical theory made it possible to base arguments upon the rate of occurrence of the commonest words in a text, scholars had seized upon the presence of *hapax legomena*, or once-occurring words, as evidence for or against hypotheses concerning authorship. In the nineteen-twenties P. N. Harrison drew attention to the large number of *hapax legomena* in the Pastoral Epistles: works which contained so many words not elsewhere found in Paul, he argued, could not be authentic works of the Apostle. In 1960 Grayston and Herdan presented a similar argument, using the same base of *hapax legomena* but a far more sophisticated statistical analysis: an analysis which, while continuing to cast doubt on the authenticity of the Pastorals, provided an argument for the homogeneity of the other

Epistles of the Pauline corpus and therefore, by implication, for their being the work of a single author.

Other authors interested in the statistical analysis of literary texts have, from time to time, used New Testament material to illustrate their methods. Thus W. Fuchs, in *Nach alle Regeln der Kunst*, compared the frequencies of various parts of speech in Luke and Acts, and in John and the Apocalypse, as a possible indicator of common or diverse authorship.

It has been claimed by a number of authors that a satisfactory stylometric approach to authorship attribution in the New Testament cannot be made on the basis of individual features selected for their real or alleged discriminatory power. A necessary preliminary to stylometric comparisons between texts must be a thorough grammatical analysis of every word in the texts to be compared. Only such an analysis will provide a reliable base for stylometric argument. This has been argued forcefully by Barbara and Timothy Friberg, of the Wycliffe Bible translators. The Fribergs themselves, by publishing in 1981 an *Analytical Greek New Testament*, containing a full parsing of each word in each text, themselves provided the base for the kind of study which they claimed to be necessary. The present book is a first attempt to make use of a full grammatical database as the foundation of a stylometric study of the New Testament.

I shall make use of the statistics of different grammatical categories, derived from the Fribergs' work, to build up a statistical picture of the regularities to be found in the New Testament writers. I shall add to the information about grammatical categories the more familiar information, readily available in modern concordances, about the frequencies of the most common words. This will enable us to present a comprehensive comparison between different works in the New Testament in respect of more than a hundred different quantifiable features of style. I shall select some ninety-nine of these for application to some of the traditional problems of authorship in the New Testament.

According to a very strong ancient tradition, Acts was written by the evangelist Luke, author of the third Gospel. According to a majority of ancient authorities, the Book of Revelation or Apocalypse, the last book of the New Testament, was written by the

Apostle John who wrote the fourth Gospel. Thirteen Epistles are attributed by name to the Apostle Paul in the New Testament; another anonymous Epistle, that to the Hebrews, has often been attributed to Paul in tradition. In the later part of this book I shall ask whether the stylometric evidence assembled supports or conflicts with the hypothesis that Luke and Acts are the work of the same author, that John and Apocalypse are by the same author, and that the thirteen Epistles of the Pauline corpus (excluding Hebrews) are by the same author.

2

Wordlists and Concordances

FOR many years, the starting-point for all those who wished to acquire statistical information about the New Testament has been Robert Morgenthaler's *Statistik des neutestamentlichen Wortschatzes* (Zurich, 1958). The kernel of that book is ninety-one pages of statistical vocabulary, in which each of the 5400 or so words of the New Testament is listed in alphabetical order, with the number of occurrences in each of the individual books. Additional tables show the proportion of vocabulary, in different books, taken up by different parts of speech, and set out frequency profiles of the New Testament as a whole and its individual parts. The favourite words of each author are also tabulated, and a complicated schema exhibits the interrelations between the vocabularies of the different books, showing how many words each has in common with none, one, two, or *N* other books in the corpus. The studies reported in the present work were begun with the aid of Morgenthaler's handbook, and some of the information in his appended tables has not yet been superseded.

In recent years, however, a number of tools of New Testament scholarship have appeared which render Morgenthaler's work partially obsolete. Morgenthaler's vocabulary list is based, for the most part, on the concordance of Moulton and Geden; the underlying New Testament text is the twenty-first edition of Nestle. In 1979 there appeared the twenty-sixth edition of Nestle, which is expected to become the *textus receptus* of the future. Morgenthaler in 1982 brought out a supplement to the third impression of his work, pointing out that the variants between the two editions of Nestle were statistically rarely of importance, and listing the alterations to his *Statistik* which would be necessary to bring it into line with the new text. But more important than the appearance of the twenty-sixth edition of Nestle was the publication of the series of fascicules of K. Aland's *Vollständige Konkordanz zum griechischen Neuen Testament*, between 1975 and 1983.

Much of the information in the massive *Vollständige Konkordanz* can be obtained, in a comparatively handy form, in the *Computer-Konkordanz zum Novum Testamentum Graece* published by the Münster Institute for the Study of the Text of the New Testament in conjunction with the computer centre of the same university. This first appeared, in partial form, in 1977, to bridge the gap, for users of the *Vollständige Konkordanz*, between the appearance of the earlier and later letters of the alphabet in the fascicules of that work. It was published as a complete work in its own right in 1980, and will no doubt be acquired by many more scholars than the few who can buy the completer work which it summarizes. It provides, moreover, the database for the second volume of the *Vollständige Konkordanz*: a volume whose title is *Spezialübersichten* and whose principal content is a 'Wortstatistik' which bids fair to replace Morgenthaler, and which was published in 1978.

The 'Wortstatistik' of the *Vollständige Konkordanz* is more accurate than Morgenthaler, without being in every way an improvement upon it. It is more accurate, because it is a computer count of a machine-readable text, whereas Morgenthaler seems to have reached his figures by a hand-count of the entries in the Moulton-Geden concordance, or, in the case of some of the more frequent words, of the entire New Testament text itself. It is also based on the more recent twenty-sixth edition of Nestle. Unlike Morgenthaler, the 'Wortstatistik' includes in its database some controverted portions of the text, such as the story of the adulteress in the Gospel of John, and both the longer and shorter endings of St Mark.

Against these improvements must be set a number of disadvantages in the new 'Wortstatistik'. In the first place, though more lavishly and expensively produced, it is much less easy to consult because of its straggling layout. Secondly, unlike Morgenthaler it does not provide the total number of words in each book, which is essential to any serious statistical study of vocabulary. Thirdly, it includes as part of its database a number of verses which appear only in the apparatus of the twenty-sixth edition of Nestle; this makes it unreliable as a wordlist of that particular text. The *Computer-*

Konkordanz, though described on its title page as 'Konkordanz zum Novum Testamentum Graece von Nestle-Aland, 26 Auflage', likewise includes references to these verses which are not part of the N26 text; but there, at least, they are marked with an asterisk. Professor F. Neirynck of Leuven, in an article 'La Nouvelle Concordance du Nouveau Testament' in *Ephemerides Theologicae Lovanienses*, has provided a useful concordance to the dubious verses which are unjustifiably included in the 'Worstatistik'. By subtracting the figures in Neirynck's table from those in the 'Worstatistik' one does, at last, arrive at a reliable statistical wordlist of the most recent standard edition of the New Testament. But the reader still needs to be on his guard against certain surprising features of the *Computer-Konkordanz* at the base. One is the treatment of crasis. If an author contracts the Greek words καί ἐγώ into κἀγώ, for instance, the passage in question will appear three times in the concordance, once under καί, once under ἐγώ, and once under κἀγώ. This is convenient for consultation of the concordance, but of course can lead to odd statistical results if it leads to the same item being counted three times.

Those who wish to compare Morgenthaler's figures with those of the new 'Worstatistik' also need to note that the two lists do not always make use of the same conventions for lemmatizing different grammatical forms under a single heading. To the English word for 'say', for instance, there correspond two Greek roots which are used in different tenses. The *Computer-Konkordanz* counts these as all occurrences of a single verb λέγω, which, occurring 2262 times, comes out as the seventh commonest word in the New Testament. In Morgenthaler's list of the most frequent words in the New Testament, on the other hand, we find in the thirteenth place λέγειν with 1318 occurrences, and in twentieth place εἰπεῖν with 925 occurrences.

Completely new possibilities for the statistical study of the New Testament were opened up by the publication, in 1981, of the *Analytical Greek New Testament* of Barbara and Timothy Friberg, of the Wycliffe Bible translators, working in association with the University of Minnesota Computer Center. This sets out the text of the third edition of the Greek New Testament (1975), which is identical in all relevant respects to that of the twenty-sixth Nestle edition, along with a grammatical tag, located below each word of the Greek text, which gives a concise grammatical analysis of the word. This annotated text is available in machine-readable form, as well as in the conventional publication by Baker Book House of Grand Rapids; and the machine-readable version of it has been made the basis of two analytical concordances, one with lexical focus, and one with grammatical focus. These have been announced for publication but have not yet appeared; however, they exist in microfiche form, and have been made available to a number of scholars including myself. The microfiche concordances of the Fribergs have been the single most useful scholarly tool in the preparation of the present book.

The concordance with the lexical focus resembles the *Vollständige Konkordanz* and the *Computer-Konkordanz* in using, as keywords, lexical items; it differs from them in two respects. First of all, the forms are not lemmatized; each occurrence of a verb in a particular mood, tense, and person counts as a separate lexical item. Secondly, each keyword, and each word of its context, appears alongside the tag which carries its grammatical analysis. Among other things, this lexical concordance provides a control on the *Computer-Konkordanz*, being produced from the same text by a different program. So far as I have checked, the figures given correspond exactly to those in the Aland 'Worstatistik' with the Neirynck correction. (For the Friberg text follows exactly the Greek New Testament, and does not include the verses from the apparatus included in the *Computer-Konkordanz* and the 'Wortstatistik'.) Neither the *Computer-Konkordanz* nor the Friberg lexical concordance includes, in general, the accentuation of the Greek text, but the *Computer-Konkordanz* does so in cases where there would otherwise be ambiguity. The Friberg concordance does not even distinguish, as keywords, between items which are homographs in the absence of readings or accents. This makes it often less convenient to use than the *Computer-Konkordanz*, though of course under a single keyword heading it is always possible to discover which of the two homographs occurs by consulting the attached grammatical tag.

It is the concordance with the grammatical focus which is the Fribergs' most original contribution to the study of the New

Testament text. In this concordance the keywords are not Greek words: they are grammatical tags. If you wish, for instance, to study the use of the optative in St Paul, or St John's use of prepositions taking the genitive, you simply look up the appropriate tags as keywords and find all the relevant passages listed in the concordance entry. The Fribergs' system of parsing is a complicated one, and looking up the right grammatical tag in the concordance is not as simple as looking up a Greek word, whether or not lemmatized; but once one has mastered the code contained in the tags, one has access to a hitherto untapped wealth of information about the frequencies of different grammatical forms and syntactical features of the New Testament.

The analytical tag which is attached to each word in the New Testament consists mainly of capital letters which are abbreviations for the relevant grammatical information. Thus, a noun that is nominative feminine and singular is accompanied by a tag reading N-NF-S; a verb in the indicative aorist active has a tag which begins VIAA. For purposes of analysis, the Fribergs divide Greek words into seven main groups: nouns, verbs, adjectives, determiners, prepositions, conjunctions, and particles. The first letter of each tag–N, V, A, D, P, C, or Q–assigns a word to one of these categories. The category of nouns includes pronouns: pronouns are tagged NP and nouns N-. The remaining parts of a noun-tag indicate the case, gender, and number of the word and, in the case of pronouns, the person. Verbs are subclassified according to mood (indicative, subjunctive, optative, imperative, infinitive, or participle). The mood is indicated by the second letter in the tag, the third indicates the tense, and the fourth the voice. The fifth and sixth places in a verb-tag provide slots for the case and gender of participles; the final two places of the eight-item tag are for the person and number. Thus VIAA--ZS marks an indicative verb in the aorist tense and active voice, in the third person singular. The category tagged A includes not only adjectives but also adverbs, which are marked AB. The determiner (D) is simply the definite article; and the Fribergs' classification of prepositions, conjunctions, and particles calls for no special explanation. The whole system of tagging is summarized in Fig. 2.1.

Table. 2.1 sets out, for the sake of illustration, the number of

ABBREVIATIONS AND SYMBOLS

N noun

P pronoun			
N nominative	M masculine	X first person	S singular
G genitive	F feminine	Y second person	P plural
D dative	N neuter	Z third person	
A accusative			
V vocative			

V verb

I indicative	P present	A active	N nominative	M masculine	X first person
S subjunctive	I imperfect	M middle	G genitive	F feminine	Y second person
O optative	F future	P passive	D dative	N neuter	Z third person
M imperative	A aorist	E either middle	A accusative		
N infinitive	R perfect	or passive	V vocative		
P participle	L pluperfect	D middle deponent			
R participle		O passive deponent			
(imperative sense)		N middle or			
		passive deponent			

S singular
P plural

A adjective

P pronominal				
B adverb				
C cardinal	N nominative	M masculine	X first person	S singular
O ordinal	G genitive	F feminine	Y second person	P plural
R relative	D dative	N neuter		
I indefinite	A accusative			
T interrogative	V vocative			

D determiner
(definite article)

N nominative	M masculine	S singular	D demonstrative
G genitive	F feminine	P plural	M comparative
D dative	N neuter		S superlative
A accusative			
V vocative			

P preposition

- G genitive
- D dative
- A accusative

C conjunction

- S subordinating
- C coordinating
- H superordinating (hyperordinating)

Q particle

- S sentential
- T interrogative
- V verbal

```
+   intertag connector
&   'and', crisis
□   function, 'used as'
/   'or'
↑   'or' (order is significant)
```

Fig. 2.1. The Friberg Analytical Scheme

Table 2.1. Parts of Speech in the
Third Epistle of John

Category	Friberg code	No. of instances	% of total
Noun	N-	32	14.6
Pronoun	NP	22	10.0
Verb	V	38	17.4
Participle	VP	11	5.0
Adjective	A	35	16.0
Adverb	AB	1	0.5
Article	D	28	12.8
Preposition	P	17	7.8
Conjunction	C	34	15.5
Particle	Q	1	0.5
TOTAL		219	

occurrences of words in each of the categories in the shortest book of the New Testament, the third Epistle of John.

As will be seen, the grammatical categories used by the Fribergs differ from the customary ones in several ways. This is in the light of a carefully worked out contemporary linguistic theory, aimed to capture discourse-level as well as sentence-level information. The analysis includes all parsing determined unambiguously by traditional Greek grammatical analysis, but also some which is determined by the context within the sentence, and some by the role of a sentence within the wider context of the discourse. The rationale of the analysis is explained in detail and carefully argued for in an appendix to the *Analytical Greek New Testament*. It is not necessary to be convinced of the appropriateness of every one of the Fribergs' classifications in order to make use of their analysis for stylometric comparison between different parts of the New Testament. As long as the same principles of classification are used for different books, rigorous comparisons can be made between them.

3

The Length of the Texts

THE most basic piece of information needed for a statistical investigation of the style of the New Testament authors is the length of the texts of the different books. Since the books differ enormously in length–the gospel of Luke is nearly a hundred times as long as the third Epistle of John–it is clear that it is the relative, not the absolute, frequency of words and grammatical features which must be studied by the stylometrician. What matters is not the raw score–the number of times, say, that the verb 'to be' appears in the fourth Gospel–but the proportion or percentage of the text which consists in occurrences of the verb. To ascertain this we clearly need to know how many words there are in the Gospel. And when we ask 'how many words?' here we are talking of tokens, not types: we are counting words as a publisher or compositor would count them, rather than counting how many distinguishable words there are in an author's vocabulary, as a lexicographer might. Vocabulary size is, of course, of interest to a stylometrist, and something will be said about it later; but it is not as basic a piece of information as the number of tokens in each text.

It is surprisingly difficult to find in works of reference the text-lengths of the New Testament books. Neither the *Computer-Konkordanz* nor the 'Wortstatistik' of Aland gives them. The Friberg concordance, in the form in which it has been available to me, gives text-lengths for some books only; but these are unusable since the grammatical tags are counted in as words on the same footing as the Greek tokens. The Computer Bible gives the text-lengths for the books which have so far appeared. But the only complete published list known to me of lengths counted by computer is by Mr M. E. Davison. It appears in an article 'Paul v. Luke: A Computer Analysis of Some Differences' in the *ALLC Bulletin* 12 (1984) 1. These figures were produced by a computer count of the Fribergs' text of the Greek New Testament on magnetic tape; they are reproduced in

Table 3.1. Length in Words of Books of the
New Testament

Book	Length	Book	Length
Matt.	18,346	Titus	659
Mark	11,304	Philem.	335
Luke	19,482	Heb.	4,953
John	15,635	Jas.	1,742
Acts	18,450	1 Pet.	1,684
Rom.	7,111	2 Pet.	1,099
1 Cor.	6,829	1 John	2,141
2 Cor.	4,477	2 John	245
Gal.	2,230	3 John	219
Eph.	2,422	Jude	461
Phil.	1,629	Apoc.	9,851
Col.	1,582	Gospels	64,787
1 Thess.	1,481	Pauline corpus	32,407
2 Thess.	823	Cath. Epistles	7,591
1 Tim.	1,591	NT	138,019
2 Tim.	1,238		

Sources
Friberg and Davison (see p. 13 above).

Table 3.1 and are the basis of the proportions and percentages given in this book.

The most easily available figures for New Testament text-lengths and vocabulary are those given in Table 3 of Morgenthaler's Appendix. These differ, sometimes quite substantially, from those used in this book, and a word should be said about the causes of the discrepancies, and the reason for preferring the Davison figures used in this book. Differences between counts of text-length may arise from differences in text counted, differences in criteria of unit, and differences in method of counting. Morgenthaler's and Davison's figures differ in all three ways. The texts differ: Morgenthaler was counting the text of Nestle 21, and omitting the adulteress pericope and the longer ending of Mark, for instance, whereas Davison was counting the Friberg text which contains all and only the displayed text of the twenty-sixth edition of Nestle which is identical in all relevant respects to the third edition of the *Greek New Testament*. Different scholars may individuate words in different ways: for instance, does 'Simon bar Jona' count as one word, two word, or three words? There are differences of this kind between the different text-length counts offered by Morgenthaler and others. Finally, Morgenthaler's results were achieved by hand-counting, whereas Davison's are the result of a computer count on a machine-readable text.

The inaccuracies in Morgenthaler's figures are candidly revealed in the way in which he sets them out. The first line of his table, for example, reads as follows:

	Wortbestand		Wortschatz
	Nestle	Statistik	
Mt	18,305	18,278	1,691

'Wortbestand' corresponds to text-length, 'Wortschatz' to vocabulary. The two figures given for text-lengths are arrived at in two different ways: the first by a hand-count of the text of Nestle, the second by totalling the occurrences of each item of vocabulary in the ninety-one pages of the vocabulary statistics (based principally on hand-counts of the concordance of Moulton-Geden). Morgenthaler is rightly proud of the close coincidence between the figures arrived at by these different means: they show a remarkable degree

Table 3.2. *Various Counts of the Text-lengths of the Epistles of the Pauline Corpus*

Source	Morgenthaler	Computer Bible	Maredsous	Friberg and Davison
Rom.	7,105	–	7,111	7,111
1 Cor.	6,811	6,803	6,828	6,829
2 Cor.	4,469	4,464	4,476	4,477
Gal.	2,229	2,219	2,230	2,230
Eph.	2,418	2,411	2,422	2,422
Phil.	1,629	1,623	1,629	1,629
Col.	1,575	1,571	1,582	1,582
1 Thess.	1,475	1,469	1,481	1,481
2 Thess.	821	817	823	823
1 Tim.	1,588	1,588	1,591	1,591
2 Tim.	1,236	1,204	1,238	1,238
Titus	658	658	659	659
Philem.	335	330	335	335

of accuracy for hand-counts carried out by an unaided individual. More surprising are the discrepancies which can occur between computer counts of the same text, such as those produced by Davison and those to be found in the computer Bible or in the publication *Bible et informatique* published from the Abbey of Maredsous. A comparison between the figures provided by the four sources is set out in Table 3.2 which gives the lengths of the Pauline Epistles according to the different counts.

The length of the entire New Testament, according to Davison's count, is 138,019; the two estimates made by Morgenthaler were 137,490 and 137,328. No figure, of course, can claim to be the uniquely accurate count; decisions about the unit of counting, and the delimitation of the text, are bound to contain an element of arbitrariness. Fortunately for the stylometrist, the differences between the results of different counts are only very rarely likely to throw up statistically significant differences between results based on different counts.

4

The Distribution of Words and Parts of Speech

IF WE are to use statistical methods to study and compare the style of different portions of the New Testament it is obviously not sufficient simply to record raw data. It is not enough to know that, say, St John's Gospel contains 271 instances of ὅτι, or that the Epistle to the Ephesians contains a sentence which is 141 words long. Clearly, we need to set these numbers in their correct context and measure them in some way against the totality of the data available for the relevant text. As a next step, we can, for instance, say that the proportion of ὅτι in St John is 0.0173 of the text, or in other words that the relative frequency of ὅτι is 1.73%; we can say that the average, or mean, length of sentence in Ephesians is 30.31 words. But even proportions and means fall short of giving the information which a statistician wants if he is to feel that he understands the underlying mathematical structure of the data he is dealing with. Two texts might each have the same average sentence length, and yet be very different in sentence pattern; one might have all its sentences roughly the same length, around the average; another might have a large number of sentences below the average, and a few extremely long ones far above the average. Again two texts might contain the same proportion of a particular word, say 'begat'; one of them might contain the word occurring fairly infrequently but at regular intervals: the other might have them all clustered together in a single passage, like the 'begat's in the first chapter of St Matthew's Gospel. In order to take account of features of this kind, what is needed is knowledge of the underlying *distribution* of the vocabulary or other linguistic structure.

Something will be said in a later chapter about sentence-length distributions. In the present chapter we will consider the nature of the distributions that underlie the study of vocabulary items, whether particular words or general classes of words such as parts of speech. Here the starting-point is the *binomial distribution*.

Everyone who has tossed a coin is familiar with the basic logic of the binomial distribution. There are only two possible outcomes of the toss of a coin, heads and tails; and if the coin is unbiased each of these outcomes is equally likely and has a probability of 0.5. Given this, we all know how to work out, with a degree of tedious effort, what the chances are of, say, two heads in two tosses, or three heads in eight tosses. The mathematics of the binomial distribution is simply the generalization of this kind of calculation, for any number of tosses or trials, and for cases where the probability of a particular outcome is not 0.5 but any other value between 0 and 1 on either side of this equiprobability. Thus it covers not only the probability of tossing coins, but of throwing, say, two sixes with four dice. What is essential to the binomial distribution is that it is concerned with binomial probabilities: that it is to say, with the probability of one out of two mutually exclusive and jointly exhaustive possible outcomes of an event.

The probability of the occurrence of a word or part of speech in a text is a binomial probability in that sense. We treat each token in a text as a binomial event or trial: going through the text from first word to last, we can ask, of each word 'Is it a noun, or not a noun?' 'Is it an instance of καί, or is it an instance of some other word?' The questions we put must be ones which have only two possible answers: 'yes' or 'no', 'success' or 'failure'. When we count the number of nouns, or the number of καίs in a text, we are counting the number of 'yes's or successes among our binomial trials.

The binomial distribution provides a mathematical formula to calculate, given the number N of trials, and p the probability of success at each outcome, the probability of a given number of successful trials. Suppose we count each word in a text as a trial, and each noun as a success. Then if we know the number of words in a portion of text and if we know the probability of each word's being a noun, we can work out the probability, a priori, that our chosen portion will contain one noun, or two nouns, or three nouns, and so on. It is easy enough to count the number of words in the portion of text, but how do we know the probability of each word's being a noun? Well, if we know the frequency of nouns in the text from which the portion has been taken, we can use that proportion as the probability. Thus, if we know that the proportion of nouns in the whole text of St John's Gospel is 17%, we can say that the probability that any given word in a short, twenty-word passage of the Gospel is a noun is 0.17. Using 20 for N, and 0.17 for p, we can use the formula for the binomial distribution* to work out the probability of a twenty-word passage containing one noun, two nouns, three nouns, and so on up to twenty nouns.

But what reason is there to believe that simply because 17% of all words in the Gospel are nouns, the probability of each word's being a noun is 17? Each time a coin is tossed, the probability of heads is 0.5; each time a die is rolled the probability of a six is 0.167. But that is because coins and dice have been designed in the way they have; in such a way that any sequence of tosses or rolls is likely to be a random sequence. But the choice of words in a literary text is surely guided by quite other considerations. What reason is there to regard a literary feature as a random variable, or to expect a sequence of words to behave like a random sequence? Apart from anything else, surely the choice of one word in a text is bound to have an influence, one way or the other, on the choice of the following words?

The answer to this question is that there is no reason, a priori, to expect words or parts of speech in a text to be distributed in accordance with any particular distribution, or to behave like random variables. By calculating the binomial distribution we learn what frequencies are likely to be observed *if* the variable feature in question does occur in accordance with the binomial distribution. Whether it does or not is an empirical matter to be discovered by recording the frequencies actually observed and comparing them with those predicted by the binomial distribution.

In fact we find that if we take portions of the text of reasonable length, say fifty words, then parts of speech are distributed in the text in accordance with the binomial distribution. Let us illustrate this in the case of the Epistle to the Philippians. This is 1,629 words long; if we ignore the last twenty-nine words we get thirty-two fifty-word sections. Table 4.1 shows the number of each part of speech in each of the sections. The parts of speech are classified in accordance with the Fribergs' schemata (N = Noun, V = Verb, A = Adjective, D = Determiner, i.e. the definite article, P = Preposition,

* $\binom{N}{r} p^r q^{N-r}$, where $q = 1 - p$.

C = Conjunction). It will be seen that for the Epistle as a whole, the proportion of nouns is 31.0%, of verbs 15.8%, of adjectives 17.3%, of articles 11.6%, of prepositions 10.3%, and of conjunctions 13.3%.

At first sight, this table seems to exhibit a chaotic state of affairs, with great and unpredictable variation between one section and

Table 4.1. Parts of Speech in Fifty-word Sections of the Epistle to the Philippians

Section	N	V	A	D	P	C
1–50	26	2	6	4	8	4
51–100	16	7	9	8	9	1
101–150	20	4	9	6	4	7
151–200	18	8	4	6	8	6
201–250	13	6	10	9	5	7
251–300	15	8	7	5	4	11
301–350	17	5	7	5	7	9
351–400	9	11	9	6	6	9
401–450	16	9	7	7	6	5
451–500	12	9	10	5	8	6
501–550	17	6	10	5	3	9
551–600	16	11	11	3	5	4
601–650	19	5	9	4	3	10
651–700	14	7	7	7	6	9
701–750	16	8	10	2	7	7
751–800	13	10	10	7	3	7
801–850	16	8	6	4	4	11
851–900	14	12	10	1	1	12
901–950	17	6	8	7	6	6
951–1000	18	10	7	5	5	5
1001–1050	20	7	6	6	8	2
1051–1100	18	7	3	11	5	6
1101–1150	8	11	12	5	6	6
1151–1200	13	10	14	5	2	6
1201–1250	17	7	9	11	3	3
1251–1300	18	7	9	8	3	4
1301–1350	14	7	13	7	4	5
1351–1400	16	4	15	8	4	3
1401–1450	8	13	10	3	6	10
1451–1500	7	17	7	3	5	11
1501–1550	15	8	9	4	5	9
1551–1600	22	4	5	8	6	4

Note

Three sections each have a single occurrence of a particle (Q).

another. Consider, for instance, the nouns. If 31% of the whole
Epistle is nouns, then the average number of nouns in a fifty-word
section must be 15.5. But sections vary widely from this, with as
many as twenty-six in the first section, and as few as seven in the
antepenultimate one. Does not this show the folly of trying to pin
down the free creative spirit of a writer within the soulless confines
of a statistical distribution?

In fact, it turns out that each of the parts of speech is distributed in
a manner closely approximating to the theoretical binomial distribution. Consider the case of prepositions: 10.3% of the total text,
the first 1,600 words of Philippians, consists of prepositions. We can
therefore use 0.103 as the probability p, with N as 50, and by sub-
stituting in the binomial formula we can calculate the probability for
different values of r, that is to say, the probability that a section will
contain a given number of prepositions. We find, by calculation, the
following results:

The likelihood that a section will contain 3 or less   is 0.229
The likelihood that a section will contain just 4   is 0.175
The likelihood that a section will contain just 5   is 0.184
The likelihood that a section will contain just 6   is 0.159
The likelihood that a section will contain 7 or more is 0.253

Since there are thirty-two sections, we multiply each of these
probabilities by thirty-two to get the theoretically expected number
of sections containing r prepositions: thus the expectation is that
7.33 (0.229 × 32) sections will contain three or less prepositions. We
can find the actual number of sections containing r prepositions by
consulting the table above. We can then compare the expected and
the actual results, which are shown in the following table:

	expected	observed
Sections with 3 or less	7.33	7
Sections with 4	5.60	4
Sections with 5	5.89	7
Sections with 6	5.09	7
Sections with 7 or more	8.10	7

It will be seen that the actual results do not differ greatly from the expected results, and that the actual distribution is reasonably close to the expected one. But there are undoubtedly differences between the two distributions, and we need to know whether to attach importance to them. In order to discover this, we have to apply another statistical test, the chi-squared test. This is a very generally useful test to determine whether the differences between a set of predicted and observed results are statistically significant, or whether they are simply the kind of differences to be expected between one hand and another fairly dealt from the same pack of cards. One common use of the chi-squared test is, as here, to test whether a set of observed results is a good fit to a theoretical distribution such as the binomial.

To calculate chi-squared for the table above, we apply the formula

$$\chi^2 = \sum \frac{(O - E)^2}{E}$$

where O is the observed figure in each line, and E the expected, and where Σ instructs us to sum the results for each line. We obtain the result 0.95. Whether this is statistically significant is to be ascertained by consulting statistical tables; it will vary with the number of degrees of freedom in the case. Here we have three degrees.* Recourse to statistical tables shows us that for three degrees of freedom a chi-square of 0.95 is totally insignificant. So our investigation shows that the actual distribution of conjunctions in the Epistle to the Philippians is a good fit to the binomial distribution.

It would be tedious to go through the calculation for the other parts of speech in the same detail. Table 4.2 shows the expected and observed values for the different parts of speech, with the respective chi-square. (Where the expected value of a particular frequency is less than five, classes have been grouped together, in accordance with the common practice of statisticians, in order to increase the

---

* The number of degrees of freedom is usually one less than the number of cells in the table; but here an extra degree of freedom is lost since the probability for each of the fifty-word sections was calculated from the proportion in the whole text.

Table 4.2. Parts of Speech in Philippians, fitted to a Binomial Distribution

(i) Nouns: $N = 50$, $p = 0.310$, mean $= 15.5$, standard deviation $= 3.27$

No. of nouns in section	Expected	Actual	Expected	Actual
12 or less	5.76	5 ⎫	8.77	8
13	3.01	3 ⎭		
14	3.58	3 ⎫	7.46	5
15	3.87	2 ⎭		
16	3.81	5 ⎫	7.23	10
17	3.42	5 ⎭		
18	2.82	3 ⎫	8.48	9
19 or more	5.66	6 ⎭		

Chi-squared 1.98 for 2 degrees of freedom; non-significant

(ii) Verbs: $N = 50$, $p = 0.158$; mean $= 7.9$, standard deviation $= 2.58$

No. of verbs in section	Expected	Actual	Expected	Actual
6 or less	9.76	9		
7	4.83	7 ⎫	9.70	12
8	4.86	5 ⎭		
9	4.26	3 ⎫	7.52	5
10	3.26	2 ⎭		
11 or more	4.99	8		

Chi-squared 3.26 for 2 degrees of freedom; non significant

(iii) Adjectives: $N = 50$, $p = 0.173$, mean $= 8.65$, standard deviation $= 2.67$
The distribution fits a binomial, chi-squared 4.85 for 2 degrees of freedom

(iv) Conjunctions: $N = 50$, $p = 0.133$; mean $= 6.65$, standard deviation $= 2.41$
The distribution fits a binomial, chi-squared 0.49 for 2 degrees of freedom

reliability of the chi-squared test.) In no case is the value of chi-square significant, and we can conclude that all the parts of speech are binomially distributed in the Epistle to the Philippians.

One may wonder whether individual words, like parts of speech, are also binomially distributed. A partial answer is already in the tables: for the definite article, while forming a class on its own, as a determiner, is also of course a single vocabulary item, the commonest word, indeed, in the Epistle. Table 4.3 shows the fit to the binomial of other common words: καί and ἐν (the second and third commonest words) and Χριστός (the commonest noun). It will

Table 4.3. Common Words in Philippians, fitted to a Binomial Distribution

(i)   The definite article: $N = 50$; $p = 0.116$; mean $= 5.8$; standard deviation $= 2.26$

No. in section	Expected	Actual	Expected	Actual
3 or less	4.90	5 ⎫		
4	4.61	4 ⎬	9.51	9
5	5.54	7		
6	5.47	4 ⎫		
7	4.51	5 ⎬	9.98	9
8 or more	7.01	7		

Chi-squared 0.51 for 2 degrees of freedom: non-significant

(ii)   The conjunction καί: $N = 50$; $p = 0.067$; mean $= 3.35$; standard deviation $= 1.77$

No. of καίs in section	Expected	Actual
1 or less	4.58	5
2	6.30	4
3	7.23	9
4	6.11	6
5 or more	7.74	8

Chi-squared 1.32 for 3 degrees of freedom: non-significant

(iii)   The preposition εν: N $= 50$; $p = 0.042$; mean $= 2.10$; standard deviation 1.42
     Chi-squared for 0.58 for 2 degrees of freedom: non-significant

(iv)   Χριστός: $N = 50$; $p = 0.023$; mean $= 1.15$; standard deviation 1.095
     Chi-squared 1.45 for one degree of freedom; non-significant

be seen that these two fit reasonably well the binomial distribution, in the fifty-word sections.

However, as p drops, and equally if N drops so that the text is divided into shorter and shorter sections, the binomial distribution cannot be expected to provide such a good fit to the data, and this for reasons both of general statistical theory and of the nature of the literary subject matter.

5

The Commonest Words

THOUGH it is the uncommon words in a text which catch the eye and attract the interest of scholars, the common words are often the most important for stylometric studies. It is not so much the rare words an author uses, as the characteristic rate of his use of the words he shares with all other writers, which often mark a text with his particular stamp.

Like most texts in Greek, or indeed any language, a large part of the New Testament is made up of repetitions of a few common words. Table 5.1 sets out the frequencies of the twenty commonest

Table 5.1. The Twenty Commonest Words in the New Testament

Greek word	Occurrences	Frequency (%)	Rough equivalent
ὁ	19,904	14.43	the
καί	9,164	6.64	and
αὐτός	5,601	4.06	he, she, it
δέ	2,801	2.03	but
ἐν	2,757	2.00	in
εἶναι	2,461	1.78	be
λέγειν	2,262	1.64	say
ὑμεῖς	1,847	1.34	you
ἐγώ	1,802	1.31	I
εἰς	1,768	1.28	to
οὐ	1,613	1.17	not
οὗτος	1,391	1.01	this
ὅς	1,365	0.99	who
θεός	1,318	0.96	God
ὅτι	1,297	0.93	that
πᾶς	1,244	0.90	all
σύ	1,066	0.77	you
μή	1,043	0.76	not
γάρ	1,042	0.76	for
Ἰησοῦς	919	0.67	Jesus

Source

Computer-Konkordanz zum Novum Testamentum Graece.

words in the New Testament. The commonest words are short, colourless words, which can be used in a variety of ways in a variety of contexts. If we count the commonest words as being those which are more frequent than the most common noun in a text, we always find that they make up a very substantial portion of the whole. Thus, in the New Testament, the most common noun is, appropriately, θεός, the Greek word for 'God', and the next most common is the name 'Jesus'. We find that about 40% of the whole text consists of words which are commoner than 'θεός' and over 45% consist of words which are commoner than 'Jesus'.

But though the same words are common in all the books, the rate at which they occur differs from book to book, and this may help to provide information concerning common or diverse authorship of different parts of the New Testament.

Table 5.2 sets out the occurrences of the conjunction καί, one of the commonest words in the New Testament or in any Greek text, in the main sections of the New Testament. After the raw score of occurrences is given the proportion of the text constituted by tokens

Table 5.2. καί in the New Testament

Work	Occurrences	Frequency (%)	Standard error
Matt.	1,194	6.51	0.18
Mark	1,099	9.72	0.28
Luke	1,482	7.61	0.19
John	866	5.54	0.18
Acts	1,130	6.12	0.18
Paul	1,569	4.84	0.12
Heb.	250	5.25	0.32
Caths.	427	5.63	0.26
Apoc.	1,126	11.43	0.32
NT	9,153	6.63	

The total includes occurrences of καί in crasis (e.g. κἄν).

Source

Aland, 'Wortstatistik' with Neirynck's correction (see p. 7).

of the word; to avoid a superfluity of noughts, the proportion (here as elsewhere in the book) is expressed as a percentage. To each percentage there is attached a standard error of the proportion. A standard error is a measure of the reliability of a sample as an indicator of the proportion in the population from which the sample is drawn. Statistical theory shows that if we have a random sample with a given proportion p then of the possible populations from which it could have been drawn approximately 68% will have proportions lying no further than one standard error away from p in either direction; approximately 95% will be distant from p by no more than $\pm$ two standard errors; and more than 99% will lie within three standard errors of p. The value of a standard error is a function both of the proportion and of the size of the sample; it is calculated by the formula: $\sqrt{pq/\text{N}}$. To give a proportion without a standard error attached is misleading: on the other hand to attach a standard error to every vocabulary frequency given in this book would be wasteful of paper. Instead, Table 5.3 sets out standard errors for various frequencies in each of the books of the New Testament. Consultation of this will reveal the approximate standard error for any vocabulary frequency.

When we are using a short text of an author as an indication of his style, we are treating it as a sample drawn from an indefinite potential population of prose homogeneous in style with it. When we are asking whether two texts are by the same author, we raise first the question whether they can both be regarded as samples drawn randomly from the same stylistically homogeneous population. If the answer is affirmative, this does not of course settle the question whether the two texts are by the same author, but it provides some evidence in favour. If the answer is in the negative, this again does not disprove common authorship; but it means that some explanation of the difference is called for (which might be, for instance, difference of subject-matter, or chronological difference, or the influence of source material). If the proportions of two texts differ by more than three times the sum of their standard errors, then it is very unlikely that the two texts can be considered as samples from a single population which is homogeneous in respect of the feature being measured.

The table shows marked differences between the rates of

Table 5.3: Standard Errors of Various Proportions in Individual Books of the New Testament

Book	Frequency of feature, expressed as a percentage												
	0.05	0.1	0.2	0.3	0.4	0.5	0.6	0.7	0.8	0.9	1.0	2.0	5.0
Matt.	0.017	0.023	0.033	0.040	0.047	0.052	0.057	0.061	0.066	0.070	0.073	0.103	0.161
Mark	0.021	0.030	0.042	0.051	0.059	0.066	0.072	0.078	0.084	0.088	0.094	0.132	0.205
Luke	0.016	0.023	0.032	0.039	0.045	0.051	0.055	0.060	0.064	0.068	0.071	0.100	0.156
John	0.018	0.025	0.035	0.044	0.050	0.056	0.061	0.067	0.071	0.076	0.079	0.112	0.174
Acts	0.016	0.023	0.033	0.040	0.046	0.052	0.057	0.061	0.065	0.070	0.073	0.103	0.160
Rom.	0.027	0.037	0.052	0.065	0.075	0.084	0.092	0.099	0.106	0.112	0.118	0.166	0.258
1 Cor.	0.027	0.038	0.054	0.066	0.076	0.085	0.093	0.101	0.108	0.114	0.120	0.169	0.264
2 Cor.	0.033	0.047	0.067	0.082	0.094	0.105	0.115	0.125	0.133	0.141	0.149	0.209	0.326
Gal.	0.047	0.067	0.095	0.116	0.134	0.149	0.164	0.177	0.189	0.200	0.211	0.296	0.462
Eph.	0.045	0.064	0.091	0.111	0.128	0.143	0.156	0.169	0.181	0.192	0.202	0.284	0.443
Phil.	0.055	0.078	0.111	0.136	0.156	0.175	0.191	0.207	0.221	0.234	0.247	0.347	0.540

	0.05	0.1	0.2	0.3	0.4	0.5	0.6	0.7	0.8	0.9	1.0	2.0	5.0
Col.	0.056	0.079	0.112	0.138	0.159	0.177	0.194	0.210	0.224	0.237	0.250	0.352	0.548
1 Thess.	0.058	0.082	0.116	0.142	0.164	0.183	0.201	0.217	0.231	0.245	0.259	0.364	0.566
2 Thess.	0.078	0.111	0.156	0.191	0.220	0.246	0.269	0.291	0.311	0.329	0.347	0.489	0.760
1 Tim.	0.056	0.079	0.112	0.137	0.158	0.177	0.194	0.209	0.223	0.236	0.249	0.351	0.546
2 Tim.	0.064	0.090	0.127	0.155	0.179	0.200	0.219	0.236	0.253	0.268	0.283	0.398	0.619
Philem.	0.122	0.173	0.244	0.298	0.345	0.385	0.422	0.456	0.487	0.516	0.544	0.765	1.191
Heb.	0.032	0.045	0.063	0.078	0.090	0.100	0.110	0.118	0.127	0.134	0.141	0.199	0.310
Jas.	0.054	0.076	0.107	0.131	0.151	0.169	0.185	0.200	0.213	0.226	0.238	0.335	0.522
1 Pet.	0.054	0.077	0.109	0.133	0.154	0.172	0.188	0.203	0.217	0.230	0.242	0.341	0.531
2 Pet.	0.067	0.095	0.135	0.165	0.190	0.213	0.233	0.251	0.269	0.285	0.300	0.432	0.657
1 John	0.048	0.068	0.097	0.124	0.136	0.152	0.167	0.180	0.193	0.204	0.215	0.303	0.471
2 John	0.143	0.202	0.285	0.349	0.403	0.450	0.493	0.533	0.569	0.603	0.636	0.894	1.390
3 John	0.151	0.214	0.302	0.370	0.427	0.477	0.522	0.563	0.602	0.638	0.672	0.946	1.473
Jude	0.104	0.147	0.208	0.255	0.293	0.329	0.360	0.389	0.415	0.440	0.463	0.652	1.015
Apoc.	0.023	0.032	0.045	0.055	0.064	0.071	0.078	0.084	0.089	0.095	0.100	0.141	0.219
Freq.	0.05	0.1	0.2	0.3	0.4	0.5	0.6	0.7	0.8	0.9	1.0	2.0	5.0

occurrence of καί in different works. Historical works, in general, score higher than Epistles, but John stands out among the evangelists as sparing in his use of καί which is below the NT average. This is in marked contrast with the Apocalypse, which is nearly twice the NT average. Only Mark, in all the books of the NT, comes anywhere near the Apocalypse rate. The difference between the rate in Luke and Acts is 1.49, which is more than three times the sum of their standard errors (1.11). This, as has been said, does not indicate necessarily a difference in authorship: it may represent, for instance, the influence of the sources used by Luke in his Gospel. (Acts also favours another conjunction τε, which it uses fifty-one times as against only nine in the Gospel.)

One can represent standard errors graphically, by marking a sample frequency on a graph as a point with a line tailing away on each side of it to the limit of three standard errors. Two samples can then be regarded as possibly coming from a single population if a horizontal line can be drawn crossing each of their lines. Figure 5.1 sets out the usage of the verb 'to be' (εἶναι) in this way, using the data presented in Table 5.4.

Table 5.4. The Verb 'to be' (εἶναι) in Sections of the New Testament

Work	Occurrences	Frequency %	Standard error
Math.	288	1.56	0.09
Mark	192	1.70	0.12
Luke	361	1.85	0.10
John	442	2.40	0.12
Acts	276	1.50	0.09
Paul	560	1.73	0.07
Heb.	54	1.09	0.15
Caths.	166	2.19	0.17
Apoc.	111	1.13	0.11
NT	2,450	1.78	0.04

Source
Morgenthaler 1958, p. 167.

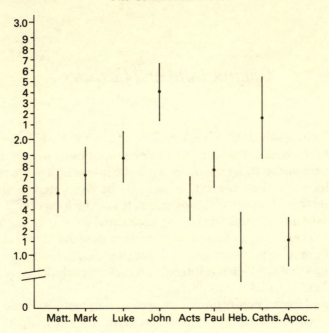

Fig. 5.1. The Verb 'to be' in the New Testament.

6

Conjunctions and Particles

THE Fribergs divide the Greek conjunctions of the New Testament into three classes. The two clauses or propositions of structures which are joined by a conjunction may be intended to have equal prominence in their context, or one may be given greater weight than another. Accordingly, the conjunctions which link them may be classed as co-ordinating (giving each equal weight), as subordinating (introducing a clause less prominent than that to which it is linked), or as hyperordinating (introducing a clause more prominent than that to which it is linked). Thus every conjunction will be tagged either CC, CS, or CH.

Some Greek conjunctions can appear only with a single tag, others bear different tags in different contexts. Thus γάρ ('for'), which supplies a cause or reason, is regarded as subordinate to the cause it explains, and is always tagged CS. δέ, on the other hand, is treated in different contexts as having co-ordinating, subordinating, or hyperordinating function and accordingly receives different tags. In an Appendix the Fribergs list all the conjunctions which can take more than one tag, and illustrate the contexts in which they are differently parsed. Thus the conjunction is tagged CC when it is disjunctive 'or' (as in 'with whom there is no change *or* turning shadow' James 1, 17) and is tagged CS when it corresponds to the comparative 'than' (as in 'The one in you is greater than the one in the world' 1 John 4, 4). Table 6.1 sets out the frequencies of the different types of conjunction, according to this classification, in the different books of the New Testament. Some occurrences are ambiguous, and these are listed separately in the table.

It will be seen that roughly every eighth word in the New Testament is a conjunction, and that nearly two-thirds of the conjunctions are co-ordinating ones. The frequency of co-ordinating conjunctions is considerably higher in the historical books than in the Epistles, no doubt in part because of the more argumentative style and

Table 6.1. Different Types of Conjunction in Books of the New Testament

Work	CH	%	CC	%	CS	%	Ambiguous	Total	% of whole text
Matt.	395	16.3	1,567	64.8	438	18.1	19	2,419	13.19
Mark	193	11.3	1,257	73.7	250	14.7	6	1,706	15.09
Luke	378	14.4	1,805	68.6	419	15.9	29	2,631	13.50
John	344	16.8	1,141	55.6	525	25.6	41	2,051	13.12
Acts	343	14.9	1,645	71.2	279	12.1	42	2,309	12.51
Paul	665	15.4	2,181	50.4	1,427	33.0	55	4,328	13.36
Heb.	81	13.3	301	49.5	224	36.8	2	608	12.28
Caths.	125	13.4	518	55.6	281	30.2	8	932	12.28
Apoc.	17	0.1	1,180	83.5	214	15.1	2	1,413	14.34
NT	2,541	13.8	11,595	63.0	4,057	22.1	204	18,397	13.33

more sophisticated syntactic structure of the latter. But the most striking figure in the column for co-ordinating conjunctions is that for the Apocalypse: the score of 83.5% is far the highest for any book of the New Testament and well ahead of the runner-up Mark. The contrast with the fourth Gospel is marked; for John scores only 55.6%, well below the Gospel average of 65.5%. In the column for hyperordination, the Apocalypse stands out even more remarkably; this kind of conjunction is extremely rare in this book, whereas all the other works are reasonably close to the New Testament average of 13.8%. (John, once again at another extreme from the Apocalypse, shows the highest score for hyperordination on this table; but individual Pauline Epistles, namely Romans, 2 Corinthians, and Galatians, exhibit higher scores.) In subordination the Epistles score consistently higher than the historical books, and in fact every individual Epistle except that of Jude has a higher score than the Gospel average of 18.5%. Once again John stands out among the Gospels, with a comparatively high score of 25.6%, and again there is a contrast with the Apocalypse, which scores lower than any other works except Mark and Jude. The final column of the table, which exhibits the total use of conjunctions in each work, calls for little comment, though it is notable that in Mark conjunctions come more than once in every seven words.

We may now turn to particular conjunctions.

In an earlier chapter we considered the distribution of the commonest of all conjunctions, καί. In the New Testament, after καί, δέ is one of the commonest Greek conjunctions; often it means simply 'and', and often it can be left untranslated. But by comparison with καί it is more usually used to draw a contrast between the two items linked; and in this respect it can be compared with the clearly contrasting conjunction ἀλλά, or 'but'. Table 6.2 sets out the frequencies of the words δέ and ἀλλά in the main sections of the New Testament. It will be seen that comparatively high scores for one conjunction in general go with comparatively low scores for the other: thus Matthew, Luke, and Acts are high in δέ and low in ἀλλά; the Catholic Epistles, with a high ἀλλά score have a relatively low δέ score and so does the fourth Gospel. The Pauline corpus stands out as having the highest ἀλλά score combined with an average δέ score; at the other extreme the Apocalypse is on its own with the lowest score for each particle. The Apocalypse frequency of only 0.07% for the use of δέ must make it nearly unique among works written in Greek. Luke and Acts appear close together in the Table, both scoring low in ἀλλά and having the two highest scores for δέ.

Table 6.2. Two Ways of Drawing a Contrast

Work	ἀλλά		δέ	
	Occurrences	Frequency (%)	Occurrences	Frequency (%)
Matt.	37	0.20	494	2.69
Mark	45	0.40	163	1.45
Luke	35	0.18	542	2.78
John	102	0.65	213	1.37
Acts	30	0.16	554	3.00
Paul	311	0.96	636	1.96
Heb.	16	0.32	71	1.43
Caths.	49	0.65	112	1.48
Apoc.	13	0.13	7	0.07
NT	638	0.46	2,792	2.03

Source

Aland, 'Wortstatistik' with Neirynck's correction (see p. 7).

Table 6.3. Linking Reasons and Consequences

	γάρ ('for')		οὖν ('therefore')		γάρ + οὖν (%)	γάρ/γάρ + οθν (%)
	Occurrences	Frequency (%)	Occurrences	Frequency (%)		
Matt.	124	0.68	56	0.31	0.99	0.69
Mark	66	0.58	6	0.05	0.64	0.92
Luke	97	0.50	33	0.17	0.67	0.75
John	64	0.40	200	1.28	1.69	0.24
Acts	80	0.43	61	0.33	0.76	0.57
Paul	454	1.40	111	0.33	1.74	0.80
Heb.	91	1.84	13	0.26	2.10	0.88
Caths.	47	0.62	13	0.16	0.78	0.78
Apoc.	16	0.16	6	0.06	0.22	0.73
NT	1,039	0.75	499	0.36	1.11	0.68

After δέ and ἀλλά we may turn to two other common conjunctions which show the logical relationship between one part of the text and the next. Table 6.3 shows the score for the conjunction γάρ and οὖν.

This table is highly interesting. It will be seen that if we take the New Testament as a whole, we find that roughly every hundredth word is a token of one of the two types γάρ or οὖν. But there are striking differences between the rates of occurrence in different portions of the whole. The differences appear to mark characteristics both of different authors and of different genres.

If we take the two words together, their combined use can be seen as a crude indicator of the writer's interest in giving reasons and drawing consequences–whether linking his own thoughts (as in arguing from premisses to conclusions) or in interpreting the actions of others (as in reasoned narrative). The use of these words, we might say, offers an index of the logicality of a given writer. The totals in the penultimate column of the table reveal wide variation here, with the author of the Epistle to the Hebrews having the highest index, 2.10%, and the author of Revelation coming bottom, with 0.22%. As we might expect, the Epistles in general appear, by this index, much more argumentative than the Gospels: for the Gospels as a whole the index is only 0.99%, less than the NT average of 1.11%;

while for the Epistles as a whole it is 1.62%, well above the average. Acts and Revelation, like the Gospels, are below the average. But within this broad divergence between historical and epistolary genres, there are much more striking differences between individual works. The low score of the Gospels is due to the synoptic writers, because John is, by this criterion, no less argumentative than Paul. And if we exclude 2 Peter (index 1.45%) the Catholic Epistles, including the Johannine ones, are all well below the NT average, and *a fortiori* below the epistolary average.

The use of γάϱ and οὖν is, of course, only a rough index of logicality; there are many other ways of drawing logical connections between one sentence and another, though none of them is of such frequent occurrence. One Greek particle which functions in this way is ἄϱα. ἄϱα in this sense occurs only four times in the Gospels, and not at all in John; it occurs twenty-seven times in the Pauline corpus, and twice in Hebrews. To add these figures would not have affected in any substantial way the picture given by the table.

If an author likes to give reasons for what he says, there are two ways he can do so. He can either state something and then give reasons ('*q*, because *p*', or '*q*, for *p*'), or he can state the reasons first, and then go on to link them to the consequences ('*p*, therefore *q*'). γάϱ functions in the first way, and οὖν in the second. The simple vocabulary preference between the two words, therefore, reveals much more than a simple preference between two near-synonyms: it reveals a preference for one form of logical process rather than another. Hence, the final column of the table, which sets out this preference (proportion of the total use of the two words taken by uses of γάϱ), is as informing as the index of logicality which precedes it. It will be seen that the great majority of writers prefer γάϱ to οὖν, and in the NT as a whole, there are about two occurrences of γάϱ for one of οὖν. But the fourth Gospel is a striking exception: within it οὖν is more than three times as common as γάϱ. Paul and John, though of roughly equal logicality, diverge strongly here: the proportion of γάϱ to οὖν in Paul is four to one. In the use of οὖν, it will be noted, the fourth Gospel is very different from the Apocalypse; the particle is twenty times more frequent in the former than in the latter.

Another way of connecting thoughts in a text is by means of the

Table 6.4. Conditional Conjunctions in the New Testament

	ἐάν		εἰ		εἰ+ἐάν (%)	ἐάν/εἰ+ἐάν (%)
	Occurrences	Frequency (%)	Occurrences	Frequency (%)		
Matt.	62	0.34	55	0.30	0.64	0.53
Mark	33	0.29	35	0.31	0.60	0.49
Luke	28	0.14	53	0.27	0.42	0.35
John	59	0.37	48	0.30	0.68	0.55
Acts	11	0.06	36	0.20	0.26	0.23
Paul	95	0.29	209	0.64	0.94	0.31
Heb.	5	0.10	16	0.32	0.42	0.24
Caths.	32	0.42	37	0.49	0.91	0.46
Apoc.	9	0.09	16	0.16	0.25	0.36
NT	334	0.24	505	0.37	0.61	0.40

Note

Occurrences of ἐάν do not include occurrences in crasis (κἄν).

conditional conjunction. Table 6.4 shows the usage of two conditional expressions in NT greek, ἐάν and εἰ, both equivalent to 'if', but followed by different grammatical constructions.

The table shows that the New Testament exhibits considerable variation both in the total use of conditional clauses (indicated by the figure in the final column) and in the preferences between the construction introduced by εἰ and that introduced by ἐάν. Paul and the Catholic Epistles stand out in their frequent use of conditionals, being some 50% above the New Testament average; Acts and Revelation are at the other extreme. The Gospels are all close to the average except for Luke, who has a low score, though not as low as Acts. When we look at the differences between the two conditional conjunctions we see that in the NT as a whole, εἰ exceeds ἐάν in the proportion of three to two. Matthew and John, however, stand out in preferring ἐάν to εἰ, and in Mark the proportions are roughly equal. Once again, Luke occupies a position between the other evangelists and Acts.

Logicians, when analysing language, group together conditionals and negatives as two ways of forming new sentences out of old sentences with which they are logically connected. In Greek, just as there are two kinds of conditional, so too there are two forms of negative, at home in different contexts.

In Greek there are two common words corresponding to 'not' in English, namely *οὐ* and *μή*. Which of the two is used depends on the syntactic context, and so a difference between the frequencies of the two words indicates a difference in preference between syntactic constructions. Table 6.5 sets out the frequencies of the two negatives in the main sections of the New Testament, and the proportion of negatives which consist of *μή*. It will be seen that the Epistles make much more frequent use of negation than the Gospels do; the Catholic Epistles, for both negatives together, have the highest score, namely 2.90%. The least negative of the works, by this criterion, is Acts, where both negations together total less than 1% of the total. Luke, similarly, is the least negative of the Gospels, with a total of 1.52%. Once again John stands out from the other Gospels, having a total for both negatives of 2.83%, nearly as high as that for the Catholic Epistles, and greater than the total for Paul or Hebrews. Once again we have a contrast between the Gospel of John and the Apocalypse: negation is more than twice as frequent in the Gospel.

Table 6.5. Negation in the New Testament

Work	*οὐ*		*μή*		*μή/οὐ + μή* (%)
	Occurrences	Frequency (%)	Occurrences	Frequency (%)	
Matt.	199	1.08	129	0.70	0.39
Mark	122	1.08	77	0.68	0.39
Luke	172	0.88	140	0.72	0.45
John	279	1.78	117	0.75	0.30
Acts	111	0.60	64	0.35	0.37
Paul	487	1.50	352	1.08	0.42
Heb.	66	1.33	40	0.81	0.38
Caths.	109	1.44	111	1.46	0.50
Apoc.	67	0.68	50	0.51	0.43
NT	1,612	1.17	1,043	0.76	0.39

Source

Aland, 'Wortstatistik'.

The contrasts are particularly marked for *οὐ*: here John has the highest score of any work, while the Apocalypse comes second lowest. In the case of *μή* it is the Catholic Epistles which stand out: this is due particularly to James and the Johannines. As for preferences between *μή* and *οὐ*, it will be seen that nowhere does the frequency of *μή* notably exceed that of *οὐ*, and that commonly there are three occurrences of *οὐ* to every two of *μή*; the Catholic Epistles are unusual in their comparative fondness for *μή*.

Having treated of connectives which show the logical connection between one clause and another, we may turn to those whose principal use is to show the purpose or result of an action or event reported. Here are the most common ones *ἵνα*, *ὅπως*, and *ὥχτε*.

Table 6.6 resembles in some ways the tables showing conjunctions for logical connection. John and Paul again stand out: they like to show purposes and results and link outcomes with their antecedents, and these particles are about twice as frequent in their writings as in the other books of the NT taken together. In this case, however, Hebrews does not align with Paul, but scores below the NT mean. When we turn from the totals in the final column to the particular particles we see that while a preference for *ἵνα* over the

Table 6.6. Purpose and Result

	Occurrences of *ἵνα*	Frequency of *ἵνα* (%)	Occurrences of *ὅπως, ὥστε*	Frequency of these (%)	combined frequency (%)
Matt.	39	0.21	32	0.17	0.39
Mark	64	0.57	24	0.13	0.69
Luke	46	0.24	11	0.06	0.29
John	145	0.93	2	0.02	0.94
Acts	15	0.08	22	0.12	0.20
Paul	247	0.76	48	0.15	0.91
Heb.	20	0.40	3	0.06	0.46
Caths.	45	0.59	4	0.05	0.65
Apoc.	42	0.43	0	0	0.43
NT	663	0.48	136	0.10	0.58

Source

Aland, 'Worstatistik'.

other two particles is very widespread, John stands out in the force of his preference: almost 99% of his use of outcome-conjunctions are uses of ἵνα. This differentiates him from Paul, where ἵνα makes up no more than 84% of the total.

The position of Acts is interesting: it is the only work in which the other methods of expressing outcome predominate over ἵνα. (This remains true if we consider all the works of the NT singly, rather than grouping the Epistles as in the table.) In this Acts differs quite strikingly from Luke. One may wonder whether to pay more attention to this than to the fact that Acts resembles Luke in having an unusually low total score for these particles. One way to check on this is to set up a contingency table comparing the two works, thus:

Work	Occurrences of ἵνα	Occurrences of ὥστε/ὅπως	Other words
Luke	46	11	19,425
Acts	15	22	18,416

To ascertain whether the differences indicated in this table are significant, one can calculate the chi-squared statistic. It comes out as 18.43. For a 3×2 contingency table of this kind, we have two degrees of freedom, and the probability of achieving a chi-square of 18.43 for two degrees of freedom is only about 0.001. We therefore conclude that there is here a significant difference between the usage in Luke and Acts. This does not, of course, mean that we can conclude that Luke and Acts are by different authors; but it shows that we have here a feature which we should consider when, in the second part of the book, we turn to consider the authorship of those two works.

If we draw up similar contingency tables, based on the figures in the main table, for the outcome particles in other works, we find that Luke and Acts each resemble Matthew more than they resemble each other (chi-squared Matthew/Luke = 11.81; Matthew/Acts = 12.74). If we introduce John into the comparison, he is seen to be extremely far removed from any of the other three (chi-squared Luke/John = 81.04; Matthew/John = 101.96; Acts/John = 143.18). As before, John stands also at a long distance from the Apocalypse: while the Apocalypse shares John's preference for ἵνα, the absolute frequency of it is twice as great in the Gospel.

We may end our consideration of conjunctions with remarks on a number of words which resist the previous classification. ὅτι and ὡς are conjunctions which have a wide variety of uses, which only in part overlap with each other. ὅτι can be used to introduce indirect speech, and also to give a cause or reason, like 'because' in English. ὡς has these uses too, but can also be used to mean 'how', or 'about', or 'as'. Both of them are multi-purpose conjunctions, and in a more detailed stylistic analysis it would be valuable to separate out the various uses in different authors. But as Table 6.7 shows, some interesting features emerge even from the crude consideration of all uses of these conjunctions blocked together.

In the use of ὅτι the fourth Gospel stands out not only in comparison with the other Gospels, but in the New Testament as a whole. The frequency of 1.74% is nearly twice that of the whole New Testament; it is approached only by the Catholic Epistles, where the high score is due almost entirely to the seventy-six occurrences in the first Johannine Epistle. As so often elsewhere, there is here a contrast between the fourth Gospel and the Apocalypse, which is well below the NT average, and indeed lower than any of the major sections of the NT except the Epistle to the Hebrews. With respect to ὡς, the opposite is the case: the Apocalypse has the highest score

Table 6.7. ὅτι and ὡς in the New Testament

Work	ὅτι		ὡς	
	Occurrences	Frequency (%)	Occurrences	Frequency (%)
Matt.	141	0.77	40	0.22
Mark	101	0.89	22	0.19
Luke	174	0.89	51	0.26
John	272	1.74	31	0.20
Acts	123	0.67	63	0.34
Paul	284	0.88	157	0.48
Heb.	18	0.36	22	0.44
Caths.	120	1.58	47	0.62
Apoc.	64	0.65	71	0.72
NT	1,297	0.94	504	0.37

Source
Aland, 'Wortstatistik'.

on the chart, double the overall average, while John is very close to the lowest score, that of Mark. It is only in Hebrews and Apocalypse that ὡς is actually more frequent than ὅτι: the ratio of ὅτι to ὡς in John is 8.8, whereas in the Apocalypse it is 0.9.

Particles are defined more narrowly in the Fribergs' system than in many Greek grammars. They are divided by them into three classes: sentential, interrogative, and verbal. The first class (QS) includes words such as 'Amen', 'Alleluia', 'Hosanna', 'Woe', 'Behold' as well as the Greek equivalents of 'yes' and 'no', and the untranslatable particles γε, δή, and μήν. Interrogative particles (QT) include ἆρα and εἰ in the appropriate context, along with the many negative ways of introducing a question. The principal verbal particle is ἄν (QV). Table 6.8 sets out the use of particles in the major sections of the New Testament. The first, third, and fifth columns give the raw scores; the second, fourth, and sixth give the percentage of all particles belonging to the individual classes. Finally there is given the total number of particles, with the percentage that this constitutes of the whole text in question.

It will be seen that particles, in the Fribergs' narrow definition, take up less than 1% of the text. Only in Matthew do they rise above 1%, though the Gospels in general make more use of them than the other books. This is no doubt due mainly to the recorded teaching of Jesus, full of sentential and interrogative particles: it will be noted

Table 6.8. Particles in Different Books of the New Testament

Work	QS	%	QT	%	QV	%	Total	% of text
Matt.	135	58	36	16	61	26	232	1.26
Mark	38	40	23	24	34	36	95	0.84
Luke	102	57	36	20	38	22	176	0.90
John	79	54	42	29	26	18	147	0.94
Acts	53	55	25	26	18	19	96	0.52
Paul	73	39	77	41	37	19	187	0.58
Heb.	7	41	4	23	6	35	17	0.36
Caths.	23	52	12	27	9	20	44	0.58
Apoc.	56	90	0	0	6	10	62	0.63
NT	570	54	255	24	235	22	1,060	0.77

that the frequency of particles in Luke is much higher than that in Acts. If we look at the different classes of particles, two things stand out. One is the high number of interrogative particles in the Pauline corpus; the other is the unique position of the Apocalypse, without a single interrogative particle, and with a higher proportion of sentential particles than any other book in the New Testament.

7
Prepositions

PREPOSITIONS present an attractive field of study for the statistical student of literature. They are easy to identify, and present few problems of classification; they appear to be topic-neutral and they occur very frequently. In the New Testament prepositions account for approximately 8% of the entire text, with over ten thousand occurrences.

Table 7.1 sets out the occurrences and frequency of prepositions in the major divisions of the New Testament, with a threefold classification into those followed by the accusative, those followed by the genitive, and those followed by the dative. The first three percentage columns show what percentage of the total of prepositions is represented by the particular class; the final percentage column shows what percentage of the total text of the work is accounted for by prepositions of all classes together.

Table 7.1. Prepositional Case Preferences in Sections of the New Testament

Work	PA	%	PG	%	PD	%	Total	% of text
Matt.	418	34.0	489	39.8	323	26.3	1,230	6.70
Mark	337	43.7	273	35.4	161	20.9	771	6.82
Luke	593	39.5	481	32.0	428	28.5	1,502	7.71
John	374	35.7	426	40.6	249	23.7	1,049	6.71
Acts	686	42.9	546	34.1	368	23.0	1,600	8.67
Paul	958	31.8	935	31.1	1,114	37.1	3,007	9.28
Heb.	181	41.4	181	41.4	75	14.2	437	8.82
Caths.	158	25.3	226	36.2	241	38.6	625	8.23
Apoc.	194	27.5	338	53.9	173	24.5	705	7.16
NT	3,899	35.7	3,895	35.6	3,133	28.7	10,927	7.92

Source
Fribergs.

If we consider prepositions together, it will be seen that all the works score reasonably close to the mean NT proportion of 7.92%; but that Epistles score more highly than Gospels, and that St Paul stands out as the most copious user of prepositions. Within the separate classes, we can mark the preference of Mark, Acts, and Hebrews for prepositions taking the accusative, the quite unusual fondness for the genitival prepositions in the Apocalypse, and the preponderance of prepositions taking the dative in Paul and in the Catholic Epistles. The specific nature of these preferences will become clearer when we turn from the general class of prepositions to the individual vocabulary items.

The ten commonest prepositions in the New Testament are, in order, ἐν, εἰς, ἐκ, ἐπί, πρός, διά, ἀπο, κατά, μετά, and περί. Between them these ten prepositions add up to 9,621 words, nearly 7% of the entire text. The frequencies of the first nine are set out in Tables 7.2-5.

ἐν, it will be seen (Table 7.2), accounts for much the greater part of the prepositions which take the dative, and εἰς provides nearly half of the instances taking the accusative. In the historical books the frequencies for ἐν do not diverge greatly from the Gospel mean

Table 7.2. The Two Commonest Prepositions in the New Testament

Work	ἐν		εἰς	
	Occurrences	Frequency (%)	Occurrences	Frequency (%)
Matt.	293	1.60	218	1.19
Mark	135	1.19	168	1.49
Luke	361	1.85	224	1.15
John	226	1.45	187	1.20
Acts	279	1.51	302	1.64
Paul	1,006	3.10	426	1.31
Heb.	65	1.31	74	1.49
Caths.	229	3.01	87	1.15
Apoc.	158	1.60	80	0.81
NT	2,752	1.99	1,766	1.28

Source
Aland, 'Wortstatistik' with Neirynck's correction.

of 1.57, but the preposition is much more popular in Epistles, and particularly so in Paul where it occurs approximately twice as frequently as in the Gospels. The columns for εἰς provide no very remarkable features, except for the low score for the Apocalypse.

ἐκ and ἀπό can both mean 'from' and it is interesting to note the preference of authors between the two (Table 7.3). In the New Testament as a whole ἐκ occurs thrice for every twice that ἀπο occurs; but Matthew, Luke, Acts, and Hebrews prefer ἀπό to ἐκ, and John shares with the Apocalypse a marked preference for ἐκ, each of them using it four times as often as ἀπό. ἐκ is indeed a favourite word of the Apocalypse; it scores twice the New Testament average, much higher even than John.

ἐπί and πρός, too, have a partial overlap of significance (Table 7.4). ἐπί is somewhat more popular in the New Testament as a whole: only John has a marked preference for πρός, using it nearly three times as often. This is in sharp contrast with the Apocalypse, which hardly ever uses πρός and has much the highest rate of ἐπί, more than twice the New Testament mean. Acts and Luke, too, score high for ἐπί, but they are fond of both prepositions, and have the two highest scores for πρός.

Table 7.3. Two Prepositions taking the Genitive Case: ἐκ *and* ἀπό

Work	ἐκ		ἀπο		ἐκ/ἐκ+ἀπό
	Occurrences	Frequency (%)	Occurrences	Frequency (%)	
Matt.	82	0.44	115	0.63	0.42
Mark	67	0.59	48	0.42	0.58
Luke	87	0.44	125	0.69	0.41
John	165	1.06	42	0.27	0.80
Acts	85	0.46	114	0.62	0.43
Paul	204	0.63	105	0.32	0.66
Heb.	21	0.42	23	0.46	0.48
Caths.	66	0.87	38	0.50	0.63
Apoc.	135	1.37	36	0.36	0.80
NT	916	0.66	646	0.47	0.59

Source
Aland, 'Wortstatistik' with Neirynck's correction.

Table 7.4. Two Prepositions taking All Three Cases: ἐπί *and* πρός

Work	ἐπί		πρός	
	Occurrences	Frequency (%)	Occurrences	Frequency (%)
Matt.	122	0.66	41	0.22
Mark	72	0.64	65	0.58
Luke	161	0.83	166	0.85
John	36	0.23	102	0.65
Acts	169	0.92	133	0.72
Paul	134	0.41	141	0.44
Heb.	29	0.59	19	0.38
Caths.	23	0.30	19	0.25
Apoc.	144	1.46	8	0.08
NT	890	0.64	699	0.51

Source
Aland, 'Wortstatistik' with Neirynck's correction.

Table 7.5 showing the prepositions followed by accusative and genetive reveals that Paul and Hebrews share διά and κατά as favoured words: in each case the preference is for διά with the genitive and κατά with the accusative. (In Paul the genitive uses of διά account for 0.62% of the total text, and the accusative uses of κατά add up to 179 of the total of 194.) μετά on the other hand is much more popular in the historical books than it is in the Epistles.

Among the prepositions which are not tabulated, a few peculiarities may be remarked. περί, with a frequency of 0.24% in the New Testament as a whole, scores highest in John (0.43%) and Hebrews (0.46%), lowest in Apocalypse (one single occurrence, 0.01%). παρά in almost every section is close to its New Testament frequency of 0.14%, except in the Apocalypse which has the lowest score of 0.03%, and John which has the highest score of 0.22%. σύν (overall frequency 0.09%) is relatively popular in Luke (0.12%), Acts (0.27%), and Paul (0.12%). ὑπέρ, whose sense overlaps with περί, is in general less frequent (0.11% overall) but is preferred to περί by Paul (0.31% v 0.16%). ὑπό, whose overall mean is 0.16%, scores at that rate in Luke, and higher in Acts (0.22%), Hebrews

Table 7.5. *Three Prepositions followed by Accusative or Genitive*: διά, κατά, μετά

Work	διά		κατά		μετά	
	Occurrences	Frequency (%)	Occurrences	Frequency (%)	Occurrences	Frequency (%)
Matt.	59	0.32	37	0.20	71	0.39
Mark	33	0.29	23	0.20	56	0.50
Luke	39	0.20	43	0.22	63	0.32
John	59	0.38	10	0.06	55	0.35
Acts	74	0.40	90	0.50	65	0.35
Paul	291	0.90	194	0.60	73	0.23
Heb.	57	1.15	41	0.82	23	0.46
Caths.	37	0.49	26	0.34	12	0.16
Apoc.	18	0.18	9	0.09	51	0.52
NT	667	0.48	473	0.34	469	0.34

Source
Aland,'Worstatistik' with Neirynck's correction.

Table 7.6. *Verbs compounded with Prepositions*

Work	All verbs as proportion of total vocabulary	Compound verbs as proportion of total vocabulary
Matt.	35.3	14.2
Mark	37.8	17.6
Luke	38.9	20.5
John	34.4	10.8
Acts	38.0	21.1
Paul	35.8	17.5
Heb.	34.8	10.7
Jas.	34.1	10.7
1 Pet.	33.4	8.5
2 Pet.	33.4	8.5
Johann.	34.5	6.0
Jude	27.3	12.5
Apoc.	33.9	4.6

Source
Morgenthaler 1958.

(0.18%), Paul (0.23%), and the Catholic Epistles (0.25%). It is not popular in the Gospels and is almost totally absent from John and the Apocalypse (each 0.02%).

Besides occurring as separate words, prepositions in Greek are very commonly used to form compound verbs out of simple verbs. Morgenthaler noticed that the use of verbs compounded with prepositions is a feature which varies greatly from one writer to another within the New Testament, as can be seen in Table 7.6. Among the historical books John uses many less of these verbs than the other writers; the figures for the pastoral and non-Pauline Epistles are comparable. The most remarkably low figure is that for the Apocalypse, with only 4.6% of the vocabulary consisting of verbs compounded with prepositions. Here the only comparable figure is the 6% for the Johannine Epistles. Luke and the Acts stand out at the other extreme, with the two highest percentages of these verbs, 20.5 and 21.1 respectively.

Morgenthaler points out that in Aramaic and Hebrew it is not possible to compound verbs with prepositions in this way, and he interprets the frequency of use of these compounds as an indication of how far a writer was at home in the Greek language. Luke and Paul, he suggests, are Hellenists accustomed to living in the Diaspora; the Johannine writings bear traces of the Semitic background of their author or authors, who write Greek as if they were writing Aramaic or Hebrew.

8

The Article

WE MAY look upon the definite article either as a vocabulary item or as part of speech. If we do the former, we find that it is much the commonest single word in each book of the New Testament. If we do the latter, we may take the opportunity to study the different forms, of case, gender, and number, which it may take: this will give us the first opportunity to investigate whether there are preferences for particular cases or genders which are characteristic of the New Testament writers.

Table 8.1 sets out the frequency of the article in different works. It will be seen that in general there is not a wide variation from the New Testament mean of 14.4%. Epistles tend to use the article less than the historical works, though Hebrews has a high score close

Table 8.1. Frequency of the Definite Article in Various Sections of the New Testament

Work	Occurrences	Frequency %	Standard error
Matt.	2,790	15.21	0.27
Mark	1,513	13.38	0.32
Luke	2,646	13.58	0.25
John	2,187	13.99	0.28
Acts	2,708	14.68	0.26
Paul	3,959	12.22	0.18
Heb.	699	14.11	0.49
Jas.	232	13.32	0.81
Petrines	325	11.68	0.61
Apoc.	1,889	19.18	0.40
NT	19,878	14.40	

Source
Aland, 'Wortstatistik' with Neirynck's correction.

to the NT average. Mark, Luke, and John do not differ significantly from one another, and the difference between the frequency in Luke and in Acts is not significant at the 1% level. The Apocalypse, on the other hand, stands out with an unprecedently high frequency of 19.18%; there is no way in which it can be regarded as coming from a common homogeneous population with the fourth Gospel.

The frequencies in Table 8.1 are taken from the 'Wortstatistik' of Aland's concordance, corrected, after Neirynck, to remove occurrences which do not occur in the text of Nestle. The

Table 8.2. Various Forms of the Article in the Entire New Testament

Form	Tag	Parsing	Occurrences	% of all articles
ὁ	DNMS	Nominative Masculine Singular	2,892	14.5
ἡ	DNFS	Nominative Feminine Singular	970	4.9
τό	DNNS	Nominative Neuter Singular	598	3.0
οἱ	DNMP	Nominative Masculine Plural	1,097	5.5
αἱ	DNFP	Nominative Feminine Plural	145	0.7
τά	DNNP	Nominative Neuter Plural	217	1.1
τόν	DAMS	Accusative Masculine Singular	1,581	7.9
τήν	DAFS	Accusative Feminine Singular	1,528	7.7
τό	DANS	Accusative Neuter Singular	1,097	5.5
τούς	DAMP	Accusative Masculine Plural	734	3.7
τάς	DAFP	Accusative Feminine Plural	340	1.7
τά	DANP	Accusative Neuter Plural	617	3.1
τοῦ	DGMS	Genitive Masculine Singular	1,918	9.6
τῆς	DGFS	Genitive Feminine Singular	1,301	6.5
τοῦ	DGNS	Genitive Neuter Singular	605	3.0
τῶν	DGMP	Genitive Masculine Plural	821	4.1
τῶν	DGFP	Genitive Feminine Plural	138	0.7
τῶν	DGNP	Genitive Neuter Plural	254	1.3
τῷ	DDMS	Dative Masculine Singular	828	4.2
τῇ	DDFS	Dative Feminine Singular	878	4.4
τῷ	DDNS	Dative Neuter Singular	412	2.1
τοῖς	DDMP	Dative Masculine Plural	460	2.3
ταῖς	DDFP	Dative Feminine Plural	203	1.0
τοῖς	DDNP	Dative Neuter Plural	167	0.8
	DV..	Vocative (all genders, nos.)	102	0.5
TOTAL			19,885	100

Source
Fribergs.

frequencies in the remaining tables in this chapter are taken from the Fribergs' concordances. It will be noticed that there are discrepancies between the figures from the two sources. This will be due to different decisions being taken when the parsing was ambiguous. Our tables include all those cases where the Fribergs tag a word with a D (for 'determiner') as the only or first tag, whether or not they also include alternative parsings by an additional tag.

Table 8.2 sets out the different forms which the tags for determiners can take, with the form of the Greek article to which they correspond, and the interpretation in the customary grammatical terminology. This is principally to illustrate the way in which the tags in the Fribergs' concordances get translated into tables in the present book. I have compiled similar tables for all the books of the New Testament, but it would be excessively tedious to reproduce them all. Instead, the information from such tables is presented in more summary form in the later tables which chart the case,

Table 8.3. Articles: Variations between Case Preferences

Work	Nominative	Accusative	Genitive	Dative	Total
Matt.	955 34.1	817 29.1	644 23.0	387 13.8	2,803
Mark	493 32.7	489 32.5	320 21.2	204 13.5	1,506
Luke	794 30.1	786 29.8	630 23.9	425 16.1	2,635
John	895 40.0	626 28.0	487 21.8	228 10.2	2,236
Acts	620 22.9	927 34.3	706 26.1	451 16.7	2,704
Paul	1,120 25.5	1,211 27.5	1,227 27.9	841 19.1	4,399
Heb.	142 21.9	219 33.2	217 32.9	82 12.4	660
Jas.	76 33.0	65 28.3	56 24.3	33 14.3	230
Petrines	71 22.1	92 28.7	100 31.2	58 18.1	321
Apoc.	562 30.3	488 26.3	621 33.5	185 10.0	1,856
NT	5,901 29.8	5,897 29.8	5,037 25.5	2,948 14.9	19,783

Note

For each case, the number of occurrences is given, followed by the percentage of all articles thereby constituted. Vocatives are omitted from this table.

Source

Fribergs.

gender, and number preferences of the different authors. But one thing will be immediately obvious from this first table. Not all the forms of the article learnt in the first painful lessons of Greek will come in equally handy when one progresses to the reading of Greek texts such as the New Testament. Investment in learning the nominative masculine singular form will be rewarded twenty times as much as investment in learning the nominative feminine plural.

Table 8.3 shows the distribution of articles by cases in different authors. There is a surprising degree of variation to be observed: one might have expected the proportions between the different cases to be a regular feature of Greek prose. In fact the only regularity which immediately meets the eye here is that the dative, in every author, is the least popular case. But among the other cases, none stands out as favourite. The nominative is the preferred case in all the Gospels, but nowhere else except James.

Table 8.4. Articles: Variations between Gender Preferences

Work	Masculine	Feminine	Neuter	Total
Matt.	1,641 58.5	662 23.6	500 17.8	2,803
Mark	832 55.2	393 26.1	281 18.7	1,506
Luke	1,450 55.0	651 24.7	534 20.3	2,635
John	1,401 62.7	450 20.1	385 17.2	2,236
Acts	1,443 53.4	747 27.6	514 19.0	2,704
Paul	1,908 43.4	1,445 32.8	1,046 23.8	4,399
Heb.	316 47.9	226 34.2	118 17.9	660
Jas.	72 31.3	108 47.0	50 21.7	230
Petrines	136 42.4	121 37.7	64 19.9	321
Apoc.	841 45.3	594 32.0	421 22.7	1,856
NT	10,313 52.1	5,503 27.8	3,967 20.1	19,783

Note

For each gender, the number of occurrences is given, followed by the percentage of all articles thereby constituted. The table does not include occurrences in the vocative case.

Source

Fribergs.

The accusative scores highest in Acts and Hebrews. In Paul, the Petrines, and in the Apocalypse, it is the genitive which is the favoured case. John resembles the Apocalypse in its sparing use of the dative.

When we turn from case to gender, set out in Table 8.4, there is greater regularity. With one exception, the rank order of the three genders is the same in every work, masculine, feminine, neuter. The exception is James, where feminine articles are markedly more frequent than masculine ones. At the other extreme from James is the writer of the fourth Gospel, whose preference for the masculine is most marked (62.7%) and who uses less feminine articles, in proportion, than any other author (20.1%). Before leaping to any conclusions about male chauvinism in St John, it is important to remember that in Greek the masculine and feminine

Table 8.5. Articles in Paul: Cross-tabulation of Gender by Case

	Masculine	Feminine	Neuter
Nominative	574	294	245
	51.6	26.4	22.0
	30.3	20.5	23.6
	13.2	6.7	5.6
Accusative	356	395	451
	29.6	32.9	37.5
	18.8	27.6	43.5
	8.2	9.1	10.3
Genitive	603	423	191
	49.5	34.8	15.7
	31.8	29.5	18.4
	13.8	9.7	4.4
Dative	362	320	150
	43.5	38.5	18.0
	19.1	22.3	14.5
	8.3	7.3	3.4

Note
The first line in each cell gives the raw score; the second, the percentage of row total; the third, the percentage of column total; the fourth, the percentage of the table total accounted for by the cell total. The table does not include vocatives, nor the articles occurring in the Epistle to Philemon.

Source
Fribergs.

genders have many other functions besides distinguishing between males and females.

One may wonder whether the probability of a word's being masculine, feminine, or neuter is at all related to the case in which it occurs. Table 8.5, which cross-tabulates gender by case in the Pauline Epistles, suggests a positive answer. The overall proportion of masculine to feminine articles in Paul is 43 : 33; but in the nominative case the ratio goes up to 52 : 26 or two to one; in the accusative case it drops to 30 : 33, with the feminine actually predominating. The nominative case is, of course, the case of the doer, the agent; the accusative case is the case for the object of the sentence, the patient which has things done to it. The neuter, in the accusative, outranks both masculine and feminine. But in the genitive, or possessive case, we are back to the ranking masculine, feminine, neuter.

Table 8.6. Articles: Variations between Number Preferences

Work	Singular		Plural	
Matt.	1,932	68.9	871	31.1
Mark	1,044	69.3	462	30.7
Luke	1,918	72.8	717	27.2
John	1,780	79.6	456	20.4
Acts	1,930	71.4	774	28.6
Paul	3,374	76.7	1,025	23.3
Heb.	467	70.8	193	29.2
Jas.	180	78.3	50	21.7
Petrines	247	76.9	74	23.1
Apoc.	1,325	71.4	531	28.6
NT	14,608	73.8	5,175	26.2

Note
For each number, the occurrences are given, followed by the percentage of all articles thereby constituted. The table does not include vocatives.

Source
Fribergs.

Nothing of striking interest emerges from Table 8.6 which sets out the number preferences: the scores for the individual works are fairly regularly distributed around the New Testament mean.

In general the study of articles suggests that genre and content have at least as important a role as authorship in explaining variations in case, gender, and number. This is further suggested if we compare individual books together. If we take Matthew and Mark, there are no statistically significant differences between them with respect either to case, gender, or number. Luke and Acts, on the other hand, while insignificantly different with respect to gender, in both other respects show significant differences: for case, chi-squared is 14.4 for three degrees of freedom, and for number 10.7 for one degree of freedom; both scores which are significant at the 1% level though not at the 0.1% level. The largest differences to be observed are those between John and the Apocalypse: for case chi-squared is 79.2 for three degrees of freedom, for gender 127.1 for two, and for number 36.9 for one.

9

Nouns and Pronouns

NOUNS form a class that is easily identifiable in the New Testament, and a word can normally be classified as such with little controversy. Proper names are counted by the Fribergs as nouns, and adjectives used substantivally are classified as adjectives. Apart from this, the tagging of nouns is straightforward: the tag for every noun begins with N-; the second place of the tag makes room for the classification NP for pronouns. In the present chapter we will consider first nouns, and then, briefly, pronouns.

Nouns in Greek are inflected for case, gender, and number. These features form the most obvious object for a general stylometric analysis of nouns. The third, fourth, and sixth places of a six-place tag in the Fribergs' analysis indicate case, gender, and number respectively. Thus a tag N-NM-S indicates a noun in the nominative masculine singular. The fifth place in the tag, always blank in the case of a noun, is to provide for the indication of person in the analysis of pronouns. (Thus NPNMZS will be a third-person pronoun in the masculine singular nominative.)

Nouns account for one-fifth of the New Testament text. Individual books vary quite markedly in the degree to which they make use of nouns. Of the text of the Petrine Epistles more than one quarter, 26.19%, is composed of nouns: this is the most noun-filled section of the New Testament. The author least given to the use of nouns is the fourth Evangelist: only 14.30% of the Gospel of John consists of nouns. As often, there is a marked contrast between this Gospel and the Apocalypse, which comes second only to the Petrines in its fondness for nouns.

Table 9.1 sets out the distribution of nouns by case, gender, and number in the New Testament as a whole. It will be seen that in every gender and number the vocative is the least frequent case. In general, the dative comes next in order of increasing frequency: the exception is the feminine plural where, surprisingly, the dative

Table 9.1. Distribution of Nouns by Case, Gender, and Number in the New Testament as a Whole

Case	Singular			Plural		
	Masc.	Fem.	Neut.	Masc.	Fem.	Neut
Nominative	3,594	1,605	724	861	252	251
Vocative	335	40	13	191	5	21
Accusative	2,544	2,598	1,178	753	582	638
Genitive	3,215	2,228	728	734	256	367
Dative	1,263	1,490	567	402	338	195

Source
Fribergs.

case is commoner than either the genitive or the nominative. If we look for the most frequent case, we find that in the masculine, whether singular or plural, it is the nominative case; in the other genders, whether singular or plural, it is the accusative. In the singular, in all genders, the genitive is the second most frequent case; in the plural the order of preference among cases varies, for no obvious reason, from gender to gender.

Table 9.2 gives the distribution of nouns by case in different sections of the New Testament. In general the pattern is similar to that observed in the case of the definite article and reported in the previous chapter. As before, the dative is the least favourite case with every author (leaving aside the vocative, which does not occur in the corresponding table for the article). In the case of nouns, as in the case of articles, Paul, Hebrews, and the Petrines favour the genitive above all others. These resemblances are not surprising: one might indeed expect the table for nouns to be almost a mirror of that for articles. But in fact there are interesting differences. Whereas in every Gospel the nominative was the preferred case for the article, the synoptic evangelists all use more accusative nouns than nominative nouns. John is the only author in the table to prefer the nominative case in nouns.

It is true, however, that the rate for the nominative is higher in the Gospels in general than in other works (with the noun as with the article, James is an exception here). Mark scores highest for the

Table 9.2. Distribution of Nouns by Case in Sections of the New Testament

Work	Nominative	Vocative	Accusative	Genitive	Dative	Total	% of text
Matt.	1,015 (28.5)	114 (3.2)	1,187 (32.0)	825 (23.2)	466 (13.1)	3,557	19.39
Mark	534 (27.1)	39 (2.0)	723 (36.6)	439 (22.3)	238 (12.1)	1,973	17.45
Luke	926 (25.7)	113 (3.1)	1,158 (32.2)	894 (24.9)	506 (14.1)	3,597	18.46
John	1,004 (38.1)	71 (2.7)	818 (31.0)	496 (18.8)	249 (9.4)	2,638	14.30
Acts	871 (21.8)	113 (2.8)	1,382 (34.5)	1,064 (26.6)	573 (14.3)	4,003	21.70
Paul	1,684 (23.0)	112 (1.5)	1,818 (24.8)	2,158 (29.5)	1,551 (21.1)	7,323	22.60
Heb.	230 (19.6)	6 (0.5)	368 (31.4)	413 (35.2)	155 (13.2)	1,172	23.66
Jas.	118 (30.7)	16 (4.2)	99 (25.8)	106 (27.6)	45 (11.7)	384	22.04
Pet.	147 (20.2)	4 (0.5)	191 (26.2)	248 (34.0)	139 (19.1)	729	26.19
Apoc.	614 (26.1)	27 (1.1)	691 (29.4)	752 (32.0)	266 (11.3)	2,350	23.86
NT	7,287 (25.7)	605 (2.1)	8,648 (30.5)	7,528 (26.6)	4,255 (15.0)	28,323	20.52

Note

The numbers in brackets after each score indicate the percentage of all nouns constituted by that score. The final column gives the percentage of the total text constituted by nouns.

accusative, and Paul scores lowest. There is a wide variation in the rate of the genitive, with Hebrews having the highest rate, almost double that of John who is the lowest scorer. Here again, as before with the article, John resembles the Apocalypse in using the dative sparingly, while differing from it markedly in nominative and genitive preferences. Paul, with nouns as with articles, is the most copious user of the dative case.

Table 9.3 sets out the information about gender and number preferences in sections of the New Testament. Whereas in the case of articles there was an almost universal preference for the masculine over the feminine and the feminine over the neuter, here not only James but also Hebrews and the Petrines provide exceptions to the ranking masculine-feminine-neuter. But once again John stands out in his extreme preference for the masculine gender and scores lower than any other author in the table in his use of feminine nouns. The Apocalypse, by contrast, scores lowest as a user of the masculine, and is well above the average in its use of the feminine. But where it stands out most markedly is in its use

Table 9.3. Distribution of Nouns by Gender and Number in the New Testament

Work	Masculine	Feminine	Neuter	Singular	Plural
Matt.	1,992 (56.0)	990 (27.8)	575 (16.2)	2,620 (73.9)	937 (26.1)
Mark	992 (50.3)	620 (31.4)	361 (18.3)	1,475 (74.8)	498 (25.2)
Luke	1,870 (52.0)	1,156 (32.1)	571 (15.9)	2,826 (78.6)	771 (21.4)
John	1,572 (59.6)	664 (25.2)	402 (15.2)	2,234 (84.7)	404 (15.3)
Acts	2,087 (52.1)	1,295 (32.4)	621 (15.5)	3,084 (77.0)	919 (23.0)
Paul	3,286 (44.9)	2,886 (39.4)	1,151 (15.7)	6,175 (84.3)	1,148 (15.7)
Heb.	485 (41.4)	518 (44.2)	169 (14.4)	927 (79.1)	245 (20.9)
Jas.	156 (40.6)	156 (40.6)	72 (18.7)	298 (77.6)	86 (22.4)
Pet.	297 (40.7)	327 (44.9)	105 (14.4)	592 (81.2)	137 (18.8)
Apoc.	918 (39.1)	862 (36.7)	570 (24.3)	1,740 (74.0)	610 (26.0)
NT	13,982 (49.0)	9,479 (34.4)	4,682 (16.3)	22,477 (79.4)	5,846 (20.6)

Note

The numbers in brackets for each score indicate the percentage of all nouns constituted by that score.

Source
Fribergs.

Table 9.4. Distribution of Pronouns by Case in Selected New Testament Works

Work	Nominative	Accusative	Genitive	Dative	Total	% of text
Matt. + Mark	260 (12.7)	534 (16.2)	648 (31.8)	598 (29.3)	2,040	6.88
Luke	205 (15.3)	413 (30.8)	417 (31.1)	307 (22.9)	1,342	6.89
John	119 (12.9)	261 (28.2)	239 (25.8)	307 (33.2)	926	5.92
Acts	78 (9.4)	300 (36.1)	253 (30.6)	198 (23.8)	830	4.50
Paul	157 (18.7)	187 (20.8)	306 (36.5)	188 (22.4)	838	2.57
Heb.	36 (16.4)	63 (28.8)	85 (38.8)	35 (16.0)	219	4.42
Apoc.	60 (11.0)	105 (19.3)	296 (54.3)	84 (15.4)	545	5.53
NT	989 (14.1)	1,896 (26.9)	2,380 (33.8)	1,772 (23.8)	7,037	5.10

Note

The numbers in brackets after each score indicate the percentage of pronouns constituted by that score. Only third-person pronouns are included. The final column gives the percentage of the total text constituted by such pronouns.

Source
Fribergs.

Table 9.5. Distribution of Pronouns by Gender and Number in Selected New Testament Works

Work	Masculine	Feminine	Neuter	Singular	Plural
Matt. + Mark	1,803 (88.4)	137 (6.7)	100 (4.9)	1,367 (67.1)	673 (32.9)
Luke	1,160 (86.4)	109 (8.1)	73 (5.4)	929 (69.2)	413 (30.7)
John	840 (90.7)	49 (5.3)	37 (4.0)	710 (76.7)	216 (23.3)
Acts	754 (90.8)	43 (5.2)	33 (4.0)	465 (56.0)	365 (44.0)
Paul	715 (85.3)	48 (5.7)	75 (8.9)	559 (66.7)	279 (33.3)
Heb.	187 (85.4)	16 (7.3)	16 (7.3)	136 (62.1)	83 (37.8)
Apoc.	384 (70.6)	108 (19.8)	53 (9.5)	353 (64.8)	192 (35.2)
NT	6,112 (86.9)	529 (7.5)	394 (5.6)	4,751 (67.5)	2,286 (32.5)

Note
The numbers in brackets after each score indicate the percentage of pronouns constituted by that score. Only third-person pronouns are included.

Source
Fribergs.

of the neuter noun, where it is nearly 50% above the mean score. This is something for which the statistics of the article did not prepare us.

Once again, the distribution by number seems to have little to tell us: we merely note that both John and Paul stand out by having a particularly strong preference for the singular over the plural.

Tables 9.4 and 9.5 set out the corresponding information for pronouns in the New Testament.

10

Adjectives and Adverbs

ADJECTIVES form a much less homogeneous class than nouns, and the grammatical analysis of them is correspondingly more complicated. The Fribergs make use of a seven-place tag for the analysis, rather than the six-place tag which was ample for nouns. The last four places, as with nouns, provide for indication of case, gender, person, and number; the first three allow specification of the particular kind of adjective in the question. Adjectives are first divided into those that are pronominal and those that are not pronominal: 'good' is not pronominal in 'the good man', but it is pronominal in 'the good', where it functions as a noun. If pronominal, an adjective is given the coding AP in the first two places of the tag; if not, it receives a hyphen in the second place. (The coding AB, on its own, is used to indicate an adverb.) The third place of the tag is used to classify adjectives as cardinal numbers (C), ordinal numbers (O), relatives (R), indefinites (I), interrogatives (T), demonstratives (D), comparatives (M), and superlatives (S). Adjectives which fall into none of these categories are standard adjectives, and are given a blank in the third place of the tag.

There is no need to explain in full detail the Fribergs' system of classification. Several of the types which they identify occur too rarely to make it worth while to incorporate them in a stylometric study. In this chapter we will concentrate on four types of adjec-. tives: those which are standard and not pronominal (taking the tag A--), those which are standard and pronominal (taking the tag AP-), those which are pronominal and relative (APR), and those which are pronominal and demonstrative (APD). We shall abbreviate these four categories to 'standard', 'pronominal', 'relative', and 'demonstrative'. The four categories make up the overwhelming majority of all words classified as adjectives in the *Analytic Greek New Testament*.

Table 10.1 shows how the various books of the New Testament

Table 10.1. Different Kinds of Adjectives in Sections of the New Testament

Work	Standard		Pronominal		Demonstrative		Relative		Total % of text
	Occurrences	%	Occurrences	%	Occurrences	%	Occurrences	%	
Matt.	457	2.49	424	2.31	193	1.05	426	2.32	8.17
Mark	340	3.01	304	2.69	96	0.85	234	2.07	8.62
Luke	440	2.26	453	2.32	222	1.14	517	2.65	8.37
John	209	1.34	308	1.97	296	1.89	422	2.70	7.90
Acts	509	2.76	414	2.24	184	1.00	506	2.74	8.74
Paul	1,205	3.73	949	2.93	350	1.08	983	3.03	10.77
Heb.	173	3.49	147	2.97	56	1.13	196	3.96	11.55
Jas.	91	5.22	49	2.81	11	0.63	37	2.12	10.78
Pet.	155	5.57	79	2.84	36	1.29	93	3.34	13.04
Apoc.	376	3.82	171	1.83	60	0.61	282	2.86	9.12
NT	3,896	2.82	3,262	2.36	1,582	1.15	3,805	2.76	9.09

Source
Fribergs.

make use of these four main kinds of adjective. It will be seen that, taking the group as a whole, the non-historical works make more use of adjectives than the Gospels and Acts. The Epistles of Peter make the most frequent use, and the Gospel of John the most sparing use, of adjectives of these kinds.

When we turn to particular kinds of adjectives, we see that it is the standard adjectives which show the greatest variation from work to work. The Petrine Epistles score at nearly twice the New Testament average, John less than half the average. The Gospels in general score less than the other works, but even among the Gospels Mark is twice as fond of adjectives as John is. In the case of pronominals most writers score close to the NT average of 2.36%, but John and Apocalypse are at the low end of the distribution, and Hebrews at the top. Demonstratives show comparatively little variation; here John is at the top end of the scale and the Apocalypse at the bottom. Hebrews stands out in its comparative fondness for relatives, and Mark is isolated in his sparing use of them.

Case preferences within standard adjectives are shown in Table 10.2.

The Fribergs assign to adverbs the analysis tag AB. Adverbs, according to their classification, make up almost 5% of the New Testament. Adverbs with the adverbial ending -ως, or with other formal adverbial characteristics, count as standard adverbs and are given the simple tag AB; so too are words that though formally other parts of speech are always used as adverbs. Five other subtypes of adverbs are recognized: comparative adverbs (like the equivalents of 'more' and 'rather'), tagged ABM; relative adverbs, which might perhaps more naturally be regarded as a type of conjunction, like the equivalent of 'when' in 'the day when God judges', tagged ABR; interrogative adverbs (ABT), like the equivalents of 'when?' and 'why?'; superlative adverbs, like the equivalent of 'most', tagged ABS; indefinite adverbs, like the equivalent of 'somehow' (ABI). Superlative and indefinite adverbs are rare, and occur only fifteen and fifty-four times respectively; in each case the majority of occurrences is provided by the Pauline corpus (10 ABSs, and 35 ABIs). The occurrences of the adverbs of the other kinds are set out in Table 10.3.

It will be seen that everywhere adverbs of the standard kind are far more frequent than the special subtypes, though of the 5,937 standard adverbs in the New Testament sixty-eight take an

Table 10.2. Distribution of Adjectives by Case in Sections of the New Testament

Work	Nominative	Accusative	Genitive	Dative	Total	% of text
Matt.	234 (51.2)	148 (32.4)	38 (8.0)	30 (7.0)	457	2.49
Mark	97 (28.5)	82 (24.1)	31 (9.1)	25 (7.3)	340	3.01
Luke	202 (45.9)	111 (25.2)	55 (12.5)	72 (16.4)	440	2.26
John	117 (56.0)	66 (31.6)	12 (5.7)	14 (6.7)	209	1.34
Acts	170 (33.4)	160 (31.4)	99 (19.4)	80 (15.7)	509	2.76
Paul	488 (40.5)	358 (29.7)	152 (12.6)	207 (17.2)	1,205	3.72
Heb.	67 (38.7)	47 (27.2)	45 (26.0)	14 (8.1)	173	3.49
Jas.	57 (62.2)	18 (19.8)	9 (9.9)	7 (7.7)	91	5.22
Pet.	42 (27.1)	58 (37.4)	31 (20.0)	24 (15.5)	155	5.57
Apoc.	172 (45.7)	126 (33.5)	45 (12.0)	33 (8.8)	376	3.82
NT	1,691 (43.4)	1,165 (29.9)	525 (13.5)	515 (13.2)	3,896	2.82

Table 10.3. *Types of Adverb in Various Sections of the New Testament*

Work	Standard		Comparative		Relative		Interrogative	
	Occurrences	%	Occurrences	%	Occurrences	%	Occurrences	%
Matt.	777	4.24	19	0.10	16	0.09	44	0.20
Mark	514	4.55	7	0.06	17	0.15	38	0.34
Luke	724	3.72	10	0.05	21	0.11	46	0.24
John	780	4.99	9	0.06	42	0.27	28	0.15
Acts	565	3.06	15	0.08	28	0.15	23	0.12
Paul	1,747	5.39	63	0.19	66	0.20	53	0.16
Heb.	251	5.07	17	0.34	3	0.06	2	0.04
Johann.	111	4.26	0	0	13	0.50	2	0.08
Apoc.	225	2.28	0	0	15	0.15	5	0.05
NT	5,937	4.30	141	0.10	230	0.17	285	0.21

Source
Fribergs.

alternative parsing as well. Most works are close to the NT average of 4.30%; St Paul is the fondest of adverbs, and the Apocalypse stands out as the most sparing in their use. Among the Gospels John makes most use of standard adverbs, coming close to the Pauline level; Luke is the least frequent user, and Acts too scores low on adverbs. Among the subtypes of adverbs there is little to remark, except that we notice that interrogative adverbs occur more frequently in Gospels than elsewhere.

11

The Verb

IN GREEK the verb is the most highly inflected part of speech: verbs have mood, tense, voice, person and number. In the Fribergs' analytical system, the tag for a verb begins with 'V', followed by three slots for mood, tense, and voice. The mood may be indicative (I), subjunctive (S), optative (O), imperative (M), infinitive (N). The tense may be present·(P), imperfect (I), future (F), aorist (A), perfect (R) or pluperfect (L). The voice may be active (A), middle (M), or passive (P); or a verb may be deponent, that is to say active in meaning but middle or passive in form. The last two places in a verb's tag indicate its person (X, Y, Z for first, second, and third) and its number (S and P for singular and plural). Thus VIPAXS would be sufficient to indicate that a verb was in the indicative present active, first person singular. In fact verbs are given an eight-place tag rather than a six-place tag. This is because the Fribergs treat participles as verbs and not, as other grammarians might have decided, as adjectives. This means that a verbal tag has to make room for the indication of the gender and case of the participle. The slot provided for this is in the fifth and sixth place of the eight-place tag; other forms of the verb carry blanks or hyphens in these places; so that a verb such as λύω would be tagged not VIPAXS but VIPA--XS.

The database provided by the tagged New Testament has already been used to provide an analysis of verbs in the New Testament. Michael E. Davison of the Queen's University of Belfast has published two articles in the *ALLC Bulletin*: 'Computer Analysis of Verb Forms in the Greek New Testament' (11 (3), 68-72) and 'Paul v. Luke: A Computer Analysis of Some Differences' (12 (1), 1-4). Some of the tables which follow are taken from Davison's article.

In his first article Davison provides a cross-tabulation of mood by tense, first for all verb forms, and then for each voice in turn.

Table 11.1. Verbs in the New Testament: Cross-tabulation of Mood by Tense

	Present	Imperfect	Future	Aorist	Perfect	Pluperfect	Total
Indicative	5,537	1,638	1,606	5,922	837	86	15,626 (55.6%)
Subjunctive	455			1,393	10		1,858 (6.6%)
Optative	23		0	45	0		68 (0.2%)
Imperative	846			763	3		1,612 (5.7%)
Infinitive	992		5	1,244	49		2,290 (8.1%)
Participle	3,583		12	2,228	688		6,491 (23.1%)
Participle (Imperative)	104			58	5		167
TOTAL	11,450 (41.1%)	1,638 (5.8%)	1,623 (5.8%)	11,653 (41.5%)	1,572 (5.6%)	86 (0.3%)	28,112 (100.0%)

Note

Blank cells represent forms which do not exist in Greek; cells marked zero represent possible forms which do not occur in the New Testament.

Source

Fribergs and Davison.

The table setting out all forms is reproduced as Table 11.1. It will be seen that the present aorist tenses predominate, accounting together for nearly 83% of all the verbs. Davison also identifies a number of 'grammatical *hapax legomena*', that is to say, a combination of mood, tense, and voice, which occurs only in a single place in the New Testament.

Davison's second article begins with a very useful table setting out the total number of verbs in each book of the New Testament. This is reproduced, in part, as Table 11.2. It will be seen that the historical books may make more use of verbs than the other books: Davison notes that the figures for the Epistles rarely rise above 20% while those for the Gospels and Acts never drop below 21%. We may observe also the contrast between John and Apocalypse: John uses verbs as frequently as anyone but Mark, while the Apocalypse scores lowest of those shown in the table (though one

Table 11.2. *Verbs in Various Books of the New Testament*

Work	Occurrences	Frequency %
Matt.	4,001	21.8
Mark	2,638	23.3
Luke	4,449	22.8
John	3,609	23.1
Acts	3,952	21.4
Paul	5,521	17.0
Heb.	921	18.6
Caths.	1,457	19.2
Apoc.	1,564	15.9
NT	28,112	20.4

Source
Fribergs and Davison.

or two of the shorter Pauline Epistles score lower). Davison is most interested in drawing a contrast between Luke (assumed to be the common author of Luke and Acts) and Paul (assumed to be the author of the thirteen books from Romans to Philemon). His tables (not reproduced here) show that Paul has a strong preference for the present tense (55.4% for all verbs, as contrasted with 32.4% for 'Luke'.) He points out also that Paul uses the subjunctive and optative moods twice as often as 'Luke': taken together they account for 9.6% of the latter, and 4.1% of the former.

I have made an independent study of the non-indicative moods in different authors and texts, and the results of this are shown in Table 11.3.

It will be seen that outside Luke, Paul, and Acts, the optative mood is very rare indeed. In his use of the subjunctive Paul stands out not only from 'Luke' but from almost all the other New Testament writers (the Johannine Epistles provide an exception); and the evangelist Luke exhibits a rate of use which is twice as high as that for the Acts of the Apostles. A similar difference marks Luke's use of the imperative in contrast to the use in Acts. Both these moods provide phenomena which need to be explained by

Table 11.3. Verbs in Sections of the New Testament: Moods other than the Indicative

Work	Subjunctive	Optative	Imperative	Infinitive
Matt.	282 (7.0)	0	126 (3.1)	122 (3.0)
Mark	205 (7.8)	1 (0.0)	173 (6.6)	200 (7.6)
Luke	243 (5.5)	11 (0.2)	322 (7.2)	400 (9.0)
John	255 (7.1)	1 (0.0)	144 (4.0)	144 (4.0)
Acts	74 (1.9)	17 (0.4)	144 (3.6)	479 (12.1)
Paul	496 (9.0)	31 (0.6)	457 (8.3)	529 (9.6)
Heb.	65 (7.1)	1 (0.0)	38 (4.1)	94 (10.2)
Johanns.	69 (12.9)	0	19 (3.5)	18 (3.4)
Apoc.	86 (5.5)	0	96 (6.1)	104 (6.6)
NT	1,858 (6.6)	68 (0.2)	1,612 (5.7)	2,290 (8.1)

Note
The figures in brackets after each frequency are the percentage of all verbs.

Source
Fribergs.

anyone who wishes, as Davison does, to regard the third Gospel and Acts as works of the same hand. The wide fluctuations from work to work in the frequency of the imperative are surprising, and not easy to explain: it is not a case of a difference of genre between historical and non-historical works, since two of the Gospels (Mark and Luke) score above the average, while the others score below; and some epistolary works, such as Hebrews, score low, while the Pauline Corpus scores high. Similar variations across genre are exhibited by the infinitive. Luke, Acts, and Paul are all at the top end of the scale, but the variation within the Gospels (Luke scoring three times as high as Matthew) is astonishingly large. The phenomena exhibited in this table clearly call for further examination.

When we turn to the indicative mood the material provided by the analytical concordance is so copious and complicated that it proved necessary to sample it rather than to treat it in its entirety. I chose to record and analyse only uses of the third-person singular of the indicative in its various moods and tenses. This is a substantial sample, made up of 8,390 verbs in the entire NT.

Comparison with Table 11.1 shows that this constitutes 53.7% of all the indicative verbs in the New Testament.

Table 11.4 sets out the distribution of these verbs by tense in different sections of the New Testament. It will be seen that the frequency of the present is generally lower in the historical books, and particularly low in Luke and Acts; the highest scorer is James, more than half of whose indicative verbs are in the present. John's score stands out as high among the Gospels; the Apocalypse is low by comparison with the other non-historical books. There are very wide variations in the use of the future; particularly noteworthy is the high score in Luke and the very low one in Acts. As if to compensate, Acts has an uncommonly high number of imperfects. Luke and Acts come together again when we turn to the aorist: they are both at the top end of the scale, using this tense more than half of the time, as does the Apocalypse. Paul and James use the aorist comparatively rarely. The perfect tense is more favoured in non-historical writing: its use is particularly characteristic of

Table 11.4. Indicative Verbs: Distribution by Tense in Sections of the New Testament

Work	Present	Future	Imperfect	Aorist	Perfect	Pluperfect	Total
Matt.	381 (30.3)	188 (15.0)	84 (6.7)	571 (45.5)	32 (2.5)	0	1,256
Mark	273 (30.3)	56 (6.2)	169 (18.7)	368 (40.8)	32 (3.5)	4 (0.4)	902
Luke	298 (19.9)	171 (11.4)	223 (14.9)	762 (50.8)	36 (2.4)	11 (0.7)	1,501
John	554 (40.2)	63 (4.6)	176 (12.8)	507 (36.8)	57 (4.1)	20 (1.5)	1,377
Acts	168 (16.6)	27 (2.7)	204 (20.1)	583 (57.6)	22 (2.2)	9 (0.9)	1,013
Paul	650 (50.6)	152 (11.8)	27 (2.1)	331 (25.8)	124 (9.7)	0	1,284
Heb	92 (38.2)	16 (6.6)	20 (8.3)	80 (33.2)	33 (13.7)	0	241
Jas.	59 (52.2)	17 (15.0)	3 (0.3)	24 (21.2)	10 (8.8)	0	113
Pet.	39 (41.5)	10 (10.6)	7 (7.4)	29 (30.9)	9 (9.6)	0	94
Apoc.	135 (29.6)	45 (9.9)	27 (5.9)	239 (52.4)	10 (2.2)	0	456
NT	2,755 (32.8)	746 (8.9)	946 (11.3)	3,250 (42.0)	375 (4.5)	45 (0.6)	8,390

Note
Only verbs in the third-person singular are included.

Source
Fribergs.

Table 11.5. Indicative Verbs: Distribution by Voice in the New Testament

Work	Active	Middle	Passive	Deponent
Matt.	926 (73.7)	25 (2.0)	157 (12.5)	148 (11.8)
Mark	685 (76.3)	35 (3.9)	66 (7.3)	112 (12.5)
Luke	1,073 (71.5)	40 (2.7)	155 (10.3)	233 (15.5)
John	1,132 (82.2)	9 (0.7)	58 (4.2)	178 (12.9)
Acts	718 (70.9)	45 (4.4)	111 (11.0)	139 (13.7)
Paul	872 (67.9)	37 (2.9)	238 (18.5)	137 (10.7)
Heb.	164 (68.0)	5 (2.1)	42 (17.4)	30 (12.4)
Jas.	69 (61.1)	5 (4.4)	15 (13.3)	24 (21.2)
Pet.	66 (70.2)	4 (4.3)	15 (16.0)	9 (9.6)
Apoc.	302 (66.2)	4 (0.9)	82 (18.0)	68 (14.9)
NT	6,188 (73.8)	180 (2.1)	957 (11.4)	1,065 (12.7)

Source
Fribergs.

Hebrews. The pluperfect, by contrast, is almost totally absent from non-historical writing: only John uses more than 1% of the time.

The distribution by voice set out in Table 11.5 seems to indicate author preferences rather than constraints of genre: most transitive active sentences, after all, can be replaced by synonymous passive ones if an author so wishes. Thus John has a very decided preference for the active over the passive, contrasting as so often with the Apocalypse which is one of the chief users of the passive, coming second only to Paul. But John and the Apocalypse share an aversion to the middle voice.

12

The Lucan Problem

TRADITIONALLY Luke has been regarded as the author of the
Acts of the Apostles, and the third Gospel has been identified with
'the former treatise' mentioned in the first words of Acts. If this is
so, we might expect to find similarities of style between the two
works. We should not expect that there will be none but statistically insignificant differences between Luke and Acts, since the
stylistic features we have been studying are likely to be influenced
by genre as well as by authorship. Since the four Gospels all deal
with the same subject-matter, and since the three synoptic
Gospels appear to draw on common material, we would expect
there to be strong similarities between Luke and the other
Gospels, as well as similarities between Luke and Acts, even if it is
the case that Acts is the work of Luke. And this is indeed what we
find. The Acts of the Apostles is closer to Luke than it is to any of
the other works of the New Testament, including the synoptic
Gospels; but Luke, while being very close to Acts, is slightly closer
to Matthew and Mark than it is to Acts.

Let us consider in turn the various features we have studied.
There is no significant difference between the rate of use of the
verb εἶναι in Luke and Acts.* Of the thirteen particles and
conjunctions whose rates we have studied individually, Luke and
Acts show no significant differences in any except three cases (καί,
μή, ἵνα).

These differences merit further study, but by themselves
provide no ground for concluding to difference of authorship.
With regard to the overall use of conjunctions, the two works differ

* For purposes of the comparisons between Luke and Acts, and John and
Apocalypse a difference is treated as significant if the rates of occurrence between
the works compared differ by more than thrice the sum of the standard errors. If a
contingency table yields a chi-square which is significant at the 0.01 level the value is
given.

insiginificantly in frequency; the division of conjunctions into different types yields a result which is just significant at the 1% level. No significant difference appears within particle use, though Luke is significantly fonder of using particles than Acts is. When we turn to prepositions we find no significant difference in overall use, or in the use of the different categories. Of the nine prepositions studied individually only one, κατά, shows a significant difference: it is over twice as common in Acts as in Luke. In respect of articles, Luke and Acts agree in overall frequency and in gender; there are differences which are just significant in the case of the number and case of articles. Acts is significantly more fond of nouns than Luke, and there are significant differences in the distribution of the case of nouns (Luke prefers the nominative to the genitive, unlike Acts); but no significant differences appear with respect to gender and number, nor in the distribution of the commonest noun θεός. In the case of pronouns, there are a number of significant differences which would repay further investigation. Acts is altogether much less fond of pronouns than Luke; there is a striking difference in the nominative, where Luke uses pronouns half as often again as Acts does.

In the case of adjectives, the usage in the two texts is much closer, both in respect of overall usage and distribution between different kinds. Within particular categories of adjectives, there are sometimes significant differences with regard to case, but never with gender or number. Both works are light on adverbs.

The most striking difference between Luke and Acts comes in the case of verbs: there are highly significant differences in the tense distribution, due principally to the much higher rate of the future in Luke. Here we have a clear case of the influence of

Table 12.1. Correlations between Features in Luke and Acts

Feature	Correlation
As	0.9737
Ds	0.9923
QPCs	0.9898
Ns	0.9965
Vs	0.9675

subject-matter and genre. Acts and Luke are both uncommonly fond of the aorist. There are no significant differences with regard to voice. Within the other moods, both Luke and Acts share a stronger preference for the infinitive than other New Testament writers, and make a use which is otherwise rare of the optative. But Luke makes very much greater use of the subjunctive, his rate of use being almost three times that of Acts.

I have been at pains to list the differences which can be detected between Luke and Acts, and the listing may have given the impression that the two works are rather different. In fact, the similarities

Table 12.2. *Significant Values of Chi-squares in Comparison between New Testament Books*

Feature	Luke-Acts	John-Rev.
Nouns		
Case	*18.7 for 4 d.f.*	*161.4 for 4 d.f.*
Gender	o	*210.6 for 2 d.f.*
Number	o	*86.3 for 1 d.f.*
Articles		
Case	14.4 for 3 d.f.	*79.2 for 3 d.f.*
Gender	o	*127.1 for 2 d.f.*
Number	10.7 for 1 d.f.	*36.9 for 1 d.f.*
Adjectives		
Case	*19.7 for 3 d.f.*	o
Gender	o	*16.2 for 2 d.f.*
Number	o	o
Relatives		
Case	15.1 for 3 d.f.	*50.7 for 3 d.f.*
Gender	o	10.0 for 2 d.f.
Number	o	*19.7 for 1 d.f.*
Demonstratives		
Case	o	o
Gender	o	o
Number	o	o
Verbs: Tense	*77.4 for 5 d.f.*	*71.8 for 5 d.f.*
Voice	o	*97.4 for 3 d.f.*

Note

A value of o is printed when the value is not significant at the 1% level. Values in italics are significant at the 0.1% level.
Fribergs.

far outweigh the differences. An indication of the closeness is given in Table 12.1, which shows how rates of occurrence of various features in Luke correlate with the rates of occurrence of the same features in Acts. The features are grouped according to the first letter of their tag in the Friberg system (see p. 10 above). The correlation figure given is a Pearson rho, which varies from 1.00 for complete positive correlation to 0 for a complete absence of correlation. It will be seen that there is a very high positive correlation in respect of all these features—adding up to some fifty independent grammatical items (individual words are not included in the base for these correlations).

Any two texts in Greek will correlate positively with each other at a significantly high level, but it is unusual for correlations to be as high as this. To show that the relationship between Luke and Acts is something much closer than could be expected by taking any two New Testament books at random, Table 12.2 shows the significance of the differences between various of the features we have been studying, in the contrasting cases of Luke-Acts and John-Apocalypse. It will be seen that not only are there twice as many significant differences in the second comparison than the first, but the size of each of the significant differences is very much greater in the Johannine cases than in the Lucan ones.

13

A Johannine Problem

WHEN we were studying the New Testament as a whole, it was rare that we found either Luke or Acts standing out at an extreme of the New Testament distribution. But both John and the Apocalypse quite often stood out as unusual. Sometimes they were together at the same end of the scale: both, for instance, avoid verbs compounded with prepositions, both score low in pronominal adjectives, and both are averse to the use of the middle voice. These and other features may be explained, as some authors have conjectured, by the two works sharing a Semitic background and an imperfect adaptation to Greek idiom.

However that may be, it is far more common to find John and Apocalypse at the opposite ends of the New Testament distribution, and certainly they are commonly on opposite sides of the New Testament mean for a particular feature. Thus, John uses nouns less than most writers, Apocalypse uses them more: there is more than an average number of indicative verbs in John, less in the Apocalypse. John is sparing with adjectives, Apocalypse uses them copiously; John likes demonstratives, and Apocalypse avoids them. John uses adverbs above the average rate, while the Apocalypse scores about half that rate. The list could be prolonged without difficulty.

We find the same contrast when we turn to the finer detail of our study. John is uncommonly fond of the verb εἶναι; Apocalypse uses it only about half as frequently. Among conjunctions, καί is more than twice as frequent in Apocalypse as in John, and of the other twelve conjunctions and particles selected for special study, there are significant differences between the rates for the two works in ten out of the twelve cases. The overall rate for conjunctions is not very different, but the distribution between the classes CC, CH, and CS is enormously different: the contingency table yields a chi-squared of 333.07 for two degrees of freedom. For the different kinds of particles the use is not so marked, but still significant: chi-squared 25.98 for two degrees of freedom.

When we turn to prepositions we find that there are a number which are used at approximately the same rates in the two works, but once again the distribution between the different categories yields a significant difference. John's preference for πρός, and Apocalypse's for ἐπί, marks them off from each other.

When studying the article we noted that the Apocalypse had much the highest rate for the whole New Testament (19.18%) while John was below the NT average of 14.4%. The distributions for case, gender, and number reveal massive differences between the works both in respect of the article and of the noun, as already exhibited in Table 12.2. John prefers the nominative to the genitive, Apocalypse has the opposite preference. John prefers the masculine very strongly to the feminine; in Apocalypse there is little difference between the frequencies of the two. Similar contrasts in gender preferences occur in several kinds of adjectives.

In verbs, there are significant differences with regard to tense and voice; there are no very striking contrasts with respect to mood. It is John's preference for the present tense which contrasts with the Apocalypse's preference for the aorist, and John's extreme preference for the active which contrasts with the Apocalypse's tolerance for the passive.

Table 13.1 shows how John and the Apocalypse correlate with each other in respect of the syntactic features that we have been studying. Beside these correlations are placed those between John

Table 13.1. Comparison between the Gospel of John and the Apocalypse

Feature	Correlation	Correlation	Correlation	Correlation
	John/Apoc.	John/Paul	Apoc./Luke	Apoc./Paul
As	0.5574	0.8711	0.8195	0.8417
Ds	0.9166	0.8911	0.8841	0.9246
QPCs	0.9309	0.9417	0.9701	0.8449
Ns	0.8998	0.9127	0.9564	0.9557
Vs	0.8686	0.9030	0.8807	0.7925

and the Pauline corpus, and those between the Apocalypse and Luke and Paul. It will be seen that in the majority of cases John correlates better with Paul than with the Apocalypse, and similarly the Apocalypse correlates better, commonly, with Luke or with Paul than with John.

We may draw together the argument of the last two chapters. From the data assembled in the earlier part of the book we can extract ninety-nine independent vocabulary and grammatical features. (The features selected are listed in the Appendix.) Using these ninety-nine features we can measure the closeness between any two books of the New Testament by seeing how the rate for each feature correlates between book and book. Table 13.2 gives the Pearson rho correlation coefficient for eight major works in the New Testament with one another.

It will be seen that according to this table Acts is closer to Luke than to any other work: the correlation between the two, in respect of these ninety-nine features, is 0.9801. Luke is closer to Mark than to any other work (0.9911) and is closer to John (0.9813) and to Matthew (0.9901) than to Acts; but it is closer to Acts than to any other work outside the Gospels.

John, on the other hand, is further away from the Apocalypse than from any other work (0.9038), and similarly the Apocalypse is further from John than from any other work. The distance between them is greater than the distance between John and Paul or between the Apocalypse and Mark. Only one distance in this table is greater: that between Mark and Paul.

Table 13.2. Pearson Correlation Coefficient for Eight Major Works in New Testament

	Matt.	Mark	Luke	John	Acts	Paul	Heb.
Mark	0.9811						
Luke	0.9901	0.9911					
John	0.9808	0.9730	0.9813				
Acts	0.9789	0.9579	0.9801	0.9544			
Paul	0.9248	0.8939	0.9256	0.9047	0.9652		
Heb.	0.9406	0.9129	0.9403	0.9145	0.9745	0.9858	
Apoc.	0.9455	0.9241	0.9349	0.9038	0.9574	0.9378	0.9472

Taken together, the arguments summarized in the last two chapters provide strong confirmation for the hypothesis that Acts was written by the same author as Luke and that John was not the author of the Apocalypse. Both of these conclusions agree with a considerable body of traditional opinion, though the second hypothesis was a minority view in antiquity, while being the prevailing one today. The interest of our argument has not been so much in providing any new or startling conclusion, but providing new and independent arguments for conclusions already reached by scholars on different grounds. My hope is that this will do something to convince scholars that the methods used are capable of reaching reasonable results in cases where there exists a scholarly consensus. The methods may then command greater respect when the conclusions to which they lead take scholars by surprise.

14

The Pauline Corpus

HITHERTO, in our tables we have given a figure for the Pauline Corpus as a whole, that is to say, for the thirteen Epistles from Romans to Philemon. This may have seemed a rash procedure, given that so many scholars regard the Pauline corpus as the work of several hands. The lumping together, however, was only provisional and the time has now come to examine the assumption of homogeneity by giving the statistics of the individual Pauline Epistles and comparing them with one another. We will study in turn the various features selected for tabulation in the New Testament as a whole.

First, as before, we look at conjunctions. Table 14.1 sets out the distribution of the different types of conjunction in the Pauline Epistles. Most of the Epistles, for the frequency of conjunctions as a whole, are fairly close to the Pauline average of 13.36% (itself close to the NT average of 13.33%). But two Epistles stand out at each end of the distribution, 1 Corinthians for its heavy use of conjunctions (2% more than its nearest Pauline competitor) and Colossians for its infrequent use (at 9.67% the lowest in the New Testament). Within the overall use Colossians again stands out as having the highest proportion of co-ordinating conjunctions and the lowest of hyperordinating.

Table 14.2 gives the Pauline frequencies of the commonest conjunction, καί. To illustrate the variability of word-counting the figures are given both from the usual source of Aland's Wortstatistik and from the Computer Bible of Morton, Michaelson, and Thompson: but the Aland figures will be used in the further analysis. It will be seen that on both counts there are very substantial differences between the frequency of καί in different Epistles. Values range from 3.92 for Romans to 6.95 for 1 Thessalonians, a range as great as that shown between the four Gospels in Table 5.2. Romans, the two Epistles to the Corinthians,

Table 14.1. Different Types of Conjunction in the Pauline Epistles

Work	CH	%	CC	%	CS	%	Ambiguous	Total	% of Text
Rom.	164	17.7	424	45.6	324	34.9	17	929	13.06
1 Cor.	142	13.1	545	50.4	376	34.8	18	1,081	15.83
2 Cor.	114	18.4	264	42.6	234	37.8	7	619	13.83
Gal.	54	17.8	137	45.1	112	36.8	1	304	13.63
Eph.	38	15.3	142	57.0	69	27.7	0	249	10.28
Phil.	33	15.3	128	59.3	51	23.6	4	216	13.26
Col.	14	9.2	101	66.0	38	24.8	0	153	9.67
1 Thess.	27	12.7	117	54.9	67	31.5	2	213	14.38
2 Thess.	12	11.0	70	64.2	25	22.9	2	109	13.24
1 Tim.	27	13.4	112	55.4	61	30.2	2	202	12.70
2 Tim.	22	16.2	80	58.8	33	24.3	1	136	10.99
Titus	9	12.2	41	55.4	23	31.1	1	74	11.23
Philem.	9	20.9	20	46.5	14	32.6	0	43	12.84

Note

The percentages in the columns following the figures for occurrences are the percentages of all conjunctions. The percentages in the final column are the percentages of the total text of each Epistle constituted by conjunctions of all types.

Source

Fribergs.

Table 14.2. Two counts of καί in the Pauline Corpus

Work	Aland		Morton		
	Occurrences	%	Occurrences	Total text	% of Text
Rom.	279	3.92			
1 Cor.	291	4.26	274	6,803	4.03
2 Cor.	208	4.65	196	4,464	4.39
Gal.	73	3.27	71	2,219	3.19
Eph.	138	5.70	137	2,411	5.68
Phil.	109	6.69	107	1,623	6.59
Col.	101	6.38	101	1,571	6.43
1 Thess.	103	6.95	99	1,469	6.74
2 Thess.	50	6.08	48	817	5.88
1 Tim.	93	5.85	92	1,588	5.79
2 Tim.	69	5.57	68	1,204	5.65
Titus	37	5.61	36	658	5.47
Philem.	18	5.37	17	330	5.15

Source

Aland, 'Wortstatistik'; Morton, Michaelson, and Thompson, *The Computer Bible*.

and Galatians all score low; their highest scorer, 2 Corinthians, is well below the lowest scorer of the rest of the corpus. Morton drew attention to this fact many years ago, and used it as one of the bases of his argument that only the first four Epistles were the genuine work of the Apostle.

Table 14.3 sets out the Pauline usage of the conjunctions that were studied in Tables 6.2 and 6.3. Colossians, it will be seen, is the lowest scorer for the first three. The high frequency of δέ in 1 Corinthians is noteworthy: it is the highest in the New Testament. Romans stands out in the same way in its preference for γάρ. In all the Epistles the score for οὖν is below the New Testament average of 0.68. Four other conjunctions, exhibited earlier in Tables 6.4 and 6.6, have their Pauline frequencies set out in Table 14.4. Galatians makes the most copious use of the conditionals; Titus and Philemon stand out for the fondness for ἵνα, which surpasses that of the evangelist John.

Table 14.5, which corresponds to Table 6.5 shows the different forms of negation in Paul. Once again, Titus is at the edge of the distribution, with a very low score for οὐ and a very high one for μή. The rates for ὅτι and ὡς are exhibited in Table 14.6, and the frequencies of the different types of particle in Table 14.7.

The study of prepositional usage in Paul is informative. Comparison of Table 14.8 with Table 7.1 shows that prepositions are much commoner in the Pauline corpus than in the New Testament generally. All but three of the Epistles score above the NT average of 7.92%, and Ephesians and Colossians have extremely high rates, closely followed by 2 Corinthians. The one real exception to the Pauline fondness for prepositions is 1 Corinthians, which has indeed the lowest rate in the New Testament as a whole. Again, comparison with Table 7.1 shows that whereas in general prepositions with the dative are the least common category, in Paul as a whole, and in the majority of the Epistles, they form the commonest category.

Table 14.9 shows that this is largely due to the Pauline fondness for ἐν, which occurs in the corpus more frequently than in any other New Testament work. Other prepositions which are favoured in the Pauline Corpus are διά, κατά, and ὑπέρ, and these are set out in the same table. It will be noticed that these

Table 14.3. Four Common Conjunctions in the Pauline Epistles

Work	ἀλλά	%	δέ	%	γάρ	%	οὖν	%
Rom.	69	0.97	148	2.08	143	2.01	48	0.68
1 Cor.	72	1.05	211	3.09	106	1.55	19	0.28
2 Cor.	68	1.51	73	1.63	75	1.68	10	0.22
Gal.	23	1.03	58	2.60	36	1.61	6	0.27
Eph.	13	0.54	20	0.83	11	0.45	7	0.29
Phil.	15	0.92	27	1.70	13	0.80	5	0.31
Col.	3	0.19	5	0.32	6	0.38	5	0.32
1 Thess.	13	0.88	15	1.01	23	1.55	2	0.14
2 Thess.	5	0.61	11	1.34	5	0.61	1	0.12
1 Tim.	12	0.75	30	1.90	13	0.82	4	0.25
2 Tim.	12	0.97	24	1.94	14	1.13	3	0.24
Titus	4	0.61	8	1.21	6	0.91	0	0
Philem.	2	0.60	6	1.79	3	0.90	1	0.30

Source
Aland, 'Wortstatistik' with Neirynck's correction.

Table 14.4. Condition, Purpose, and Result in the Pauline Epistles

Work	ἐάν	%	εἰ	%	ἵνα	%	ὅπως, ὥστε	%
Rom.	20	0.28	44	0.62	30	0.42	8	0.11
1 Cor.	47	0.69	64	0.94	57	0.83	15	0.22
2 Cor.	7	0.16	36	0.80	44	0.98	9	0.20
Gal.	7	0.31	21	0.94	17	0.76	6	0.26
Eph.	1	0.04	4	0.17	23	0.95	0	
Phil.	0		13	0.80	12	0.74	3	0.18
Col.	4	0.25	4	0.25	13	0.82	0	
1 Thess.	2	0.14	1	0.07	7	0.47	3	0.20
2 Thess.	1	0.12	2	0.24	7	0.85	3	0.36
1 Tim.	3	0.19	13	0.82	15	0.94	0	
2 Tim.	3	0.24	4	0.32	5	0.40	0	
Titus	0		1	0.15	13	1.97	0	
Philem.	0		2	0.60	4	1.19	1	0.30

Source
Aland, 'Wortstatistik'.

Table 14.5. Negation in the Pauline Epistles

Work	οὐ	%	μή	%	μή/οὐ+μή
Rom.	122	1.72	80	1.13	0.40
1 Corr.	156	2.28	96	1.41	0.38
2 Corr.	93	2.08	50	1.12	0.35
Gal.	37	1.66	24	1.08	0.39
Eph.	11	0.45	16	0.66	0.59
Phil.	13	0.80	6	0.37	0.32
Col.	8	0.51	10	0.63	0.56
1 Thess.	18	1.22	15	1.01	0.45
2 Thess.	8	0.97	11	1.34	0.58
1 Tim.	9	0.57	24	1.51	0.72
2 Tim.	12	0.97	4	0.32	0.25
Titus	1	0.15	14	2.12	0.93
Philem.	0	0	2	0.60	1.00

Source
Aland, 'Wortstatistik' with Nierynck's correction.

Table 14.6. ὅτι and ὡς in the Pauline Corpus

Work	ὅτι	%	ὡς	%
Rom.	56	0.79	21	0.30
1 Cor.	60	0.88	38	0.56
2 Cor.	51	1.14	31	0.69
Gal.	29	1.30	9	0.40
Eph.	13	0.54	16	0.66
Phil.	21	1.29	7	0.43
Col.	6	0.38	7	0.44
1 Thess.	13	0.88	9	0.61
2 Thess.	11	1.34	4	0.49
1 Tim.	12	0.75	4	0.25
2 Tim.	7	0.57	5	0.40
Titus	1	0.15	2	0.30
Philem.	4	1.19	4	1.19

Source
Aland, 'Wortstatistik' with Neirynck's correction.

Table 14.7. *Different Types of Particles in the Pauline Epistles*

Work	QS	QT	QV	Total	% of text
Rom.	20	16	8	44	0.62
1 Cor.	11	46	14	71	1.04
2 Cor.	20	10	6	36	0.80
Gal.	6	1	6	13	0.58
Eph.	3	0	0	3	0.12
Phil.	3	2	1	6	0.37
Col.	2	0	2	4	0.25
1 Thess.	2	1	0	3	0.20
2 Thess.	0	0	0	0	0
1 Tim.	4	0	0	4	0.25
2 Tim.	1	1	0	2	0.13
Titus	0	0	0	0	0
Philem.	1	0	0	1	0.30

Note

The final column shows the percentage of the total text of each Epistle constituted by particles of all kinds.

Source

Fribergs.

characteristically Pauline prepositions occur with particular frequency in the Epistles of the Captivity, Ephesians, Philippians, and Colossians, whose authenticity is often called into question.

It is also possible to identify a group of prepositions which are rarer in the Pauline corpus than elsewhere: ἀπό, ἐπί, μετά, and περί (Table 14.10). Other prepositions occur with roughly the same frequency in the Pauline corpus as in the rest of the New Testament, and their frequencies are set out in Table 14.11. Finally, Table 14.12 sets out the data for the usage of verbs compounded with prepositions.

The tables setting out the use of the articles in the Pauline Epistles show an astonishing degree of diversity. First of all, in Table 14.13 the percentage of the text composed of articles ranges from 16.18 in Colossians (the highest in the New Testament, except for the Apocalypse) to 10.00 in 1 Timothy, the lowest in the New Testament. Secondly, case preferences vary greatly: compare

Table 14.8. Prepositional Case Preferences in the Pauline Epistles

Work	PA	%	PG	%	PD	%	Total	% of text
Rom.	236	(36.3)	221	(33.9)	194	(29.8)	651	9.15
1 Cor.	126	(28.4)	130	(29.3)	187	(42.2)	443	6.49
2 Cor.	156	(31.3)	160	(32.1)	183	(36.7)	499	11.15
Gal.	73	(34.9)	89	(42.6)	47	(22.5)	209	9.37
Eph.	89	(32.0)	60	(21.6)	129	(46.4)	278	11.48
Phil.	50	(29.1)	46	(26.7)	76	(44.2)	172	10.56
Col.	44	(15.1)	51	(26.6)	97	(50.5)	192	12.14
1 Thess.	46	(30.1)	44	(28.8)	63	(41.2)	153	10.33
2 Thess.	27	(30.7)	34	(38.6)	27	(30.7)	88	10.69
1 Tim.	37	(30.6)	36	(29.8)	48	(39.7)	121	7.61
2 Tim.	43	(35.5)	39	(32.2)	39	(32.2)	121	9.77
Titus	19	(38.0)	17	(34.0)	14	(28.0)	50	7.59
Philem.	13	(43.3)	7	(23.3)	10	(33.3)	30	8.96

Note

The percentages in the brackets are the percentages of all prepositions constituted by a particular case. The percentage in the final column is the percentage of the entire text constituted by all prepositions.

Source
Fribergs.

Table 14.9. Prepositions favoured in the Epistles of the Pauline Corpus

Work	ἐν	%	διά	%	κατά	%	ὑπέρ	%
Rom.	173	2.43	91	1.28	50	0.70	17	0.24
1 Cor.	171	2.50	42	0.62	24	0.35	10	0.15
2 Cor.	160	3.57	45	1.01	26	0.58	34	0.76
Gal.	41	1.84	19	0.85	17	0.76	4	0.18
Eph.	122	5.04	21	0.87	24	0.99	10	0.41
Phil.	66	4.05	14	0.86	11	0.68	7	0.43
Col.	88	5.56	14	0.88	14	0.88	7	0.44
1 Thess.	55	3.71	10	0.68	0	0	2	0.14
2 Thess.	26	3.16	10	1.22	4	0.49	2	0.24
1 Tim.	44	2.77	6	0.38	6	0.38	3	0.19
2 Tim.	37	2.99	12	0.75	7	0.44	0	0
Titus	13	1.97	3	0.46	8	1.21	1	0.15
Philem.	10	2.99	4	1.19	3	0.90	3	0.90

Source
Aland, 'Wortstatistik' with Neirynck's correction.

Table 14.10. *Prepositions less favoured in the Pauline Corpus*

Work	ἀπό	%	ἐπί	%	μετά	%	περί	%
Rom.	24	0.34	31	0.44	6	0.08	6	0.08
1 Cor.	9	0.14	19	0.30	9	0.14	10	0.16
2 Cor.	17	0.38	24	0.54	7	0.16	2	0.04
Gal.	8	0.36	8	0.36	7	0.31	0	0
Eph.	4	0.17	11	0.45	7	0.29	2	0.08
Phil.	4	0.25	7	0.43	7	0.43	4	0.25
Col.	9	0.57	6	0.38	2	0.13	4	0.25
1 Thess.	9	0.61	6	0.41	3	0.20	8	0.54
2 Thess.	8	0.97	4	0.49	5	0.61	5	0.61
1 Tim.	3	0.19	8	0.50	9	0.57	4	0.25
2 Tim.	7	0.57	6	0.48	6	0.48	3	0.24
Titus	2	0.30	2	0.30	4	0.60	3	0.45
Philem.	1	0.30	2	0.60	1	0.30	1	0.30

Source
Aland, 'Wortstatistik' with Neirynck's correction.

Table 14.11. *Some Common Prepositions in the Pauline Corpus*

Work	εἰς	%	ἐκ	%	πρός	%
Rom.	119	1.67	60	0.84	17	0.24
1 Cor.	39	0.57	34	0.50	24	0.35
2 Cor.	78	1.74	30	0.67	33	0.74
Gal.	30	1.35	35	1.57	9	0.40
Eph.	37	1.53	8	0.33	16	0.66
Phil.	23	1.41	10	0.61	4	0.25
Col.	19	1.20	11	0.70	6	0.34
1 Thess.	26	1.76	6	0.41	13	0.88
2 Thess.	14	1.70	1	0.12	4	0.49
1 Tim.	19	1.19	2	0.13	5	0.31
2 Tim.	18	1.45	7	0.57	7	0.57
Philem.	2	0.60	0	0	3	0.90

Source
Aland, 'Wortstatistik' with Neirynck's correction.

Table 14.12. Verbs compounded with Prepositions in the Pauline Corpus

Work	All verbs as proportion of total vocabulary	Compound verbs as proportion of total vocabulary
Rom.	35.3	15.5
1 Cor.	36.4	13.3
2 Cor.	35.7	14.2
Gal.	38.4	16.1
Eph.	29.8	12.6
Phil.	30.6	10.8
Col.	31.8	12.0
1 Thess.	35.1	12.1
2 Thess.	33.5	10.8
1 Tim.	31.8	11.2
2 Tim.	30.1	10.2
Titus	24.1	9.3
Philem.	23.4	6.1

Source
Morgenthaler 1958.

Table 14.13. Distribution of Articles by Case in the Pauline Epistles

Work	Nominative	Accusative	Genitive	Dative	Total	% of Text
Rom.	298 (27.1)	285 (25.9)	288 (26.2)	230 (20.9)	1,101	15.48
1 Cor.	297 (34.2)	221 (25.4)	194 (22.3)	157 (18.1)	869	12.72
2 Cor.	148 (26.4)	140 (25.0)	169 (30.1)	104 (18.5)	561	12.53
Gal.	69 (25.3)	75 (27.5)	85 (31.1)	44 (16.1)	273	12.24
Eph.	61 (14.2)	132 (30.8)	151 (35.2)	85 (19.8)	429	17.71
Phil.	40 (20.7)	79 (40.9)	40 (20.7)	34 (17.6)	193	11.85
Col.	42 (16.4)	70 (27.3)	92 (35.9)	52 (20.3)	256	16.18
1 Thess.	41 (21.2)	67 (34.7)	56 (29.0)	29 (15.0)	193	13.03
2 Thess.	30 (26.5)	20 (17.7)	38 (33.6)	25 (22.1)	113	13.73
1 Tim.	39 (24.5)	40 (25.2)	56 (35.2)	24 (15.1)	159	10.00
2 Tim.	32 (21.2)	56 (37.1)	34 (22.5)	29 (19.2)	151	12.20
Titus	16 (24.2)	17 (25.8)	14 (21.2)	19 (28.8)	66	10.02
Philem.	7 (20.0)	9 (25.7)	10 (28.6)	9 (25.7)	35	10.45

Note
The figures in brackets are the proportion of all articles constituted by the score in each case. The percentage in the final column is the proportion of the entire text constituted by articles in all cases.

Source
Fribergs.

the preference for the nominative in 1 Corinthians with that for the
genitive in Ephesians and Colossians and that for the dative in
Titus. Similarly with gender and number, in Table 14.14: note the
strength of the feminine in 2 Corinthians and in the Pastorals, and
the most unusual fondness for the neuter in Philippians. How odd
it is that Titus, the one Epistle in which the feminine surpasses the
masculine, and the plural reaches two-thirds the frequency of the
singular, should be an Epistle addressed to a singular male!

As with articles, so with nouns and pronouns (Tables 14.15-18).
No clear pattern emerges. Individual Epistles stand out with
respect to particular preferences, but there is no Epistle or set of
Epistles which regularly diverges from a common pattern among
the rest. In the case of pronouns, for instance, the most striking
feature of the table is the high rate of use in Romans and
Ephesians, which contrasts with the generally low rate of use in
Paul (less than half the NT average of 5.10). But these two Epistles
are very rarely found together in respect of other indicators.

In the case of adjectives, however, there is one pattern to be

Table 14.14. *Distribution of Articles by Gender and Number in the Pauline Epistles*

Work	Masculine	Feminine	Neuter	Singular	Plural
Rom.	484 (44.0)	364 (33.1)	253 (23.0)	887 (80.6)	214 (19.4)
1 Cor.	411 (47.3)	211 (24.3)	247 (28.4)	667 (76.8)	202 (23.2)
2 Cor.	210 (37.4)	216 (38.5)	135 (24.1)	447 (79.7)	114 (20.3)
Gal.	125 (45.8)	81 (25.7)	67 (24.5)	199 (72.9)	74 (27.1)
Eph.	175 (40.8)	149 (34.7)	105 (24.5)	313 (73.0)	116 (27.0)
Phil.	59 (30.6)	61 (31.6)	73 (37.8)	144 (74.6)	49 (25.4)
Col.	102 (39.8)	93 (36.3)	61 (23.8)	187 (73.0)	69 (27.0)
1 Thess.	100 (51.8)	55 (28.5)	38 (19.7)	141 (73.1)	52 (26.9)
2 Thess.	56 (49.6)	39 (34.5)	18 (15.0)	97 (85.8)	16 (14.2)
1 Tim.	75 (47.2)	67 (42.1)	17 (10.7)	111 (69.8)	48 (30.2)
2 Tim.	68 (45.0)	64 (42.4)	19 (12.6)	117 (77.5)	34 (22.5)
Titus	30 (45.5)	32 (48.5)	4 (6.1)	39 (59.1)	27 (40.9)
Philem.	13 (37.1)	13 (27.1)	9 (25.7)	25 (71.4)	10 (28.6)

Note

The figures in brackets are the proportion of all articles constituted by the score
for each case.

Source

Fribergs.

Table 14.15. Distribution of Nouns by Case in the Pauline Epistles

Work	Nominative	Vocative	Accusative	Genitive	Dative	Total	%
Rom.	414 (24.4)	19 (1.1)	447 (26.3)	516 (30.4)	304 (17.9)	1,700	23.91
1 Cor.	438 (31.9)	25 (1.8)	323 (23.5)	332 (24.2)	256 (18.6)	1,374	20.12
2 Cor.	185 (20.5)	4 (0.4)	221 (24.5)	278 (30.8)	215 (23.8)	903	20.17
Gal.	139 (27.6)	14 (2.8)	106 (21.1)	161 (32.0)	83 (16.5)	503	22.56
Eph.	111 (18.0)	7 (1.1)	150 (24.3)	197 (31.9)	153 (24.8)	618	25.52
Phil.	56 (15.3)	10 (2.7)	95 (25.9)	113 (30.8)	93 (25.3)	367	22.53
Col.	67 (17.2)	6 (1.5)	89 (22.9)	117 (30.1)	110 (28.3)	389	24.59
1 Thess.	57 (18.0)	14 (4.4)	71 (22.4)	97 (30.6)	78 (24.6)	317	21.40
2 Thess.	36 (17.9)	7 (3.5)	33 (16.4)	82 (40.8)	43 (21.4)	201	24.42
1 Tim.	76 (18.7)	4 (1.0)	111 (27.3)	123 (30.2)	93 (22.9)	407	25.58
2 Tim.	63 (20.3)	1 (0.3)	102 (32.9)	76 (24.5)	68 (21.9)	310	25.04
Titus	23 (15.0)	0	49 (32.0)	47 (30.7)	34 (22.2)	153	23.22
Philem.	19 (23.5)	2 (2.5)	21 (25.9)	19 (23.4)	20 (24.7)	81	24.2

Note

The numbers in brackets after each score indicate the percentage of all nouns constituted by that score. The final column gives the percentage of the total text constituted by nouns.

Source

Fribergs.

Table 14.16. Distribution of Nouns by Gender and Number in the Pauline Epistles

Work	Masculine	Feminine	Neuter	Singular	Plural
Rom.	744 (43.8)	675 (39.7)	281 (16.5)	1,479 (87.0)	221 (13.0)
1 Cor.	639 (46.5)	463 (33.7)	272 (19.8)	1,137 (82.8)	237 (17.2)
2 Cor.	348 (38.5)	417 (46.2)	138 (15.3)	756 (83.7)	147 (16.3)
Gal.	261 (51.9)	151 (30.0)	91 (18.1)	407 (80.9)	96 (19.1)
Eph.	240 (38.8)	267 (43.2)	111 (18.0)	528 (85.4)	90 (14.6)
Phil.	182 (49.6)	135 (36.8)	50 (13.6)	324 (88.3)	43 (11.7)
Col.	161 (41.4)	176 (45.2)	52 (13.4)	328 (84.3)	61 (15.7)
1 Thess.	166 (52.4)	115 (36.3)	36 (11.4)	264 (83.3)	53 (16.7)
2 Thess.	105 (52.2)	75 (37.3)	21 (10.4)	183 (91.0)	18 (9.0)
1 Tim.	179 (44.0)	188 (46.2)	40 (9.8)	314 (77.1)	93 (22.9)
2 Tim.	142 (45.8)	132 (42.6)	36 (11.6)	265 (85.5)	45 (14.5)
Titus	70 (45.8)	66 (43.1)	17 (11.1)	116 (75.8)	37 (24.2)
Philem.	49 (60.5)	26 (32.1)	6 (7.4)	74 (91.4)	7 (8.6)

Note

The numbers in brackets after each score indicate the percentage of nouns constituted by that score.

Source

Fribergs.

Table 14.17. Distribution of Pronouns by Case in the Pauline Epistles

Work	Nominative	Accusative	Genitive	Dative	Total	% of text
Rom.	40 (16.7)	55 (23.0)	93 (38.9)	51 (21.9)	239	3.36
1 Cor.	47 (32.8)	23 (16.1)	46 (32.1)	27 (18.9)	143	2.09
2 Cor.	18 (20.0)	14 (15.6)	34 (37.8)	24 (26.7)	90	2.01
Gal.	15 (24.2)	14 (22.6)	14 (22.6)	19 (30.6)	62	2.78
Eph.	9 (10.1)	16 (18.0)	48 (53.9)	16 (18.0)	89	3.67
Phil.	2 (5.9)	14 (41.2)	10 (29.4)	8 (23.1)	34	2.08
Col.	4 (18.9)	9 (20.0)	19 (42.2)	13 (28.9)	45	2.84
1 Thess.	10 (30.3)	6 (18.2)	12 (36.4)	5 (15.2)	33	2.23
2 Thess.	3 (12.0)	7 (28.0)	8 (32.0)	7 (18.0)	25	3.04
1 Tim.	6 (23.1)	7 (26.9)	4 (15.4)	9 (34.6)	26	1.63
2 Tim.	2 (6.1)	12 (36.4)	13 (39.4)	6 (18.2)	33	2.48
Titus	1 (6.7)	6 (40.0)	5 (33.3)	3 (20.0)	15	2.28
Philem.	0	4	0	0	4	1.19

Note

The numbers in brackets after each score indicate the percentage of pronouns constituted by that score. Only third-person pronouns are included. The final column gives the percentage of the total text constituted by such pronouns.

Source
Fribergs.

Table 14.18. Distribution of Pronouns by Gender and Number in the Pauline Epistles

Work	Masculine	Feminine	Neuter	Singular	Plural
Rom.	205 (85.8)	17 (7.1)	17 (7.1)	149 (62.3)	90 (37.1)
1 Cor.	118 (82.5)	12 (8.4)	13 (9.1)	100 (69.9)	43 (30.1)
2 Cor.	82 (91.1)	0	8 (8.9)	53 (58.9)	37 (41.1)
Gal.	44 (71.0)	4 (6.5)	14 (22.6)	44 (71.0)	18 (29.0)
Eph.	76 (85.4)	4 (4.5)	9 (10.1)	75 (84.3)	14 (15.7)
Phil.	29 (85.3)	1 (2.9)	4 (11.8)	27 (79.4)	7 (20.6)
Col.	39 (86.7)	4 (8.9)	2 (4.4)	41 (91.1)	4 (8.9)
1 Thess.	30 (90.9)	2 (6.1)	1 (3.0)	19 (57.8)	14 (42.4)
2 Thess.	23 (92.0)	0	2 (8.0)	16 (64.0)	9 (36.0)
1 Tim.	20 (76.9)	3 (11.5)	3 (11.5)	7 (26.9)	19 (73.1)
2 Tim.	32 (97.0)	1 (3.0)	0	20 (60.6)	13 (39.4)
Titus	14 (93.3)	0	1 (6.7)	4 (26.7)	11 (73.3)
Philem.	3 (75.0)	0	1 (25.0)	4	0

Note

The numbers in brackets after each score indicate the percentage of pronouns constituted by that score. Only third-person pronouns are included.

Source
Fribergs.

seen. This is the strikingly high frequency of adjectives, and especially standard adjectives, in the Pastoral Epistles (Tables 14.9 and 14.20).

If one examines the list of *hapax legomena* which authors have used in order to prove that the Pastorals were not written by Paul, one finds that the greater number of them are in fact descriptive adjectives. The Pastorals do not, however, as Table 14.2 shows, have a particular preference for adverbs.

Finally, Tables 14.22-26 set out the data concerning verbs in the Pauline corpus. Paul uses verbs more sparingly than most of the New Testament authors, and none of the Epistles reaches the NT average of 20.4%; the most verbal of the Epistles is 1 Corinthians with 19.2%. Apart from the brief Philemon, Ephesians is the lowest scorer: here as elsewhere Ephesians shows a Pauline feature to an exaggerated degree.

Paul's preference for the present over the aorist was remarked on by Davison in his study of verbs in Luke and Acts. With one exception, all the Epistles show a use of the subjunctive above the NT average, and Paul is the only NT author other than Luke-Acts to use the optative. Though in general Paul uses the infinitive more often than other writers, there are some surprising variations between Epistles (compare, for instance, Ephesians with Colossians, two Epistles usually very close to each other).

If we wish to make a comprehensive assessment of the homogeneity of the Pauline corpus, there are two ways in which we may proceed. We may take a single Epistle—Romans, say, or Galatians—and declare that this is, by definition, the work of Paul; and we can then take any divergence from this paradigm Epistle as indicating a difference of authorship. This method seems flawed: for if it should turn out that all the Epistles differed from our paradigm, but resembled each other fairly closely, then conclusion should surely not be that Paul wrote only Romans, while someone else wrote the other twelve Epistles. It would surely make more sense to conclude that it was Romans which was inauthentic. For 'Paul' for our purposes is the person who wrote all, or most, of the Epistles attributed to him. If there is no one person who wrote any substantial portion of the Epistles, then no one has a greater claim than any one else to be called the author Paul.

Table 14.19. *Different Kinds of Adjective in the Pauline Epistles*

Work	Standard		Pronominal		Demonstrative		Relative		Total (%)
	Occurrences	%	Occurrences	%	Occurrences	%	Occurrences	%	
Rom.	215	3.02	199	2.80	83	1.17	245	2.45	9.44
1 Cor.	218	3.21	292	4.28	85	1.24	172	2.51	11.24
2 Cor.	138	3.08	102	2.28	47	1.05	118	2.64	9.05
Gal.	46	2.11	44	1.97	22	0.99	73	3.27	8.34
Eph.	85	3.51	75	3.10	18	0.74	73	3.01	10.36
Phil.	60	3.68	53	3.25	18	1.10	73	3.01	11.04
Col.	58	3.67	42	2.65	10	0.63	63	3.98	10.93
1 Thess.	37	2.50	34	2.30	7	0.47	25	1.69	6.96
2 Thess.	23	2.79	13	1.58	6	0.73	26	3.16	8.26
1 Tim.	138	8.67	49	3.07	22	1.38	55	3.46	16.58
2 Tim.	81	6.54	22	1.78	21	1.70	43	3.47	13.49
Titus	96	14.57	17	2.58	8	1.21	13	1.97	20.33
Philem.	10	2.99	7	2.08	3	0.89	4	1.19	7.15

Source
Fribergs.

Table 14.20. Distribution of Adjectives by Case in the Pauline Epistles

Work	Nominative	Accusative	Genitive	Dative	Total	% of text
Rom.	94 (43.7)	63 (29.3)	25 (40.9)	33 (15.3)	215	3.02
1 Cor.	128 (58.7)	51 (23.4)	15 (6.9)	24 (11.0)	218	3.21
2 Cor.	51 (37.0)	35 (25.4)	24 (17.4)	28 (20.3)	138	3.08
Gal.	27 (58.7)	12 (26.1)	2 (4.3)	5 (10.9)	46	2.11
Eph.	32 (37.6)	21 (24.7)	11 (12.9)	21 (24.7)	85	3.51
Phil.	25 (41.7)	18 (30.0)	6 (10.0)	11 (18.3)	60	3.68
Col.	17 (29.3)	18 (31.0)	4 (6.9)	19 (32.8)	58	3.67
1 Thess.	8 (21.6)	7 (18.9)	8 (21.6)	14 (37.8)	37	2.50
2 Thess.	3 (13.0)	5 (21.7)	8 (34.8)	7 (30.4)	23	2.79
1 Tim.	36 (26.1)	53 (38.4)	24 (17.4)	25 (18.1)	138	8.67
2 Tim.	42 (51.9)	23 (28.4)	8 (9.88)	8 (9.88)	81	6.54
Titus	24 (25.0)	48 (50.0)	14 (14.5)	10 (10.42)	96	14.57
Philem.	1 (10.0)	4 (40.0)	3 (30.0)	2 (20.0)	10	2.99

Note

The figures in brackets are the proportion of all adjectives constituted by the score for each case. The percentage in the final column is the proportion of the entire text constituted by adjectives in all cases.

Source

Fribergs.

Table 14.21. Adverbs in the Pauline Epistles

Work	Standard adverbs	% of text	Other adverbs	% of text
Rom.	380	5.34	42	0.59
1 Cor.	434	6.36	47	0.69
2 Cor.	278	6.21	30	0.67
Gal.	138	6.19	9	0.40
Eph.	79	3.26	7	0.29
Phil.	86	5.28	15	0.92
Col.	54	3.41	5	0.32
1 Thess.	92	6.21	6	0.41
2 Thess.	40	4.86	3	0.36
1 Tim.	75	4.71	10	0.81
2 Tim.	51	4.12	5	0.40
Titus	28	4.25	0	0
Philem.	12	3.58	2	0.60

Source

Fribergs.

Table 14.22. Verbs in the Pauline Epistles

Epistle	Occurrences	Frequency (%)
Rom.	1,168	16.4
1 Cor.	1,309	19.2
2 Cor.	764	17.1
Gal.	415	18.6
Eph.	327	13.5
Phil.	256	15.7
Col.	236	14.9
1 Thess.	243	16.4
2 Thess.	121	14.7
1 Tim.	298	18.7
2 Tim.	226	18.3
Titus	114	17.3
Philem.	44	13.1
Paul	5,521	17.0

Source
Davison.

The better method is surely to start with the corpus of Pauline writings handed on by tradition, and ask whether within that corpus there is any Epistle, or group of Epistles, which is marked out as different from the body as a whole. This we are now in a position to do. We can take the features we have studied hitherto and combine them together. In the case of the Pauline corpus ninety-six out of the ninety-nine features listed in the Appendix can be used to compare the Epistles. Table 14.27 sets out the correlations, Epistle by Epistle. This enables us to make a solidly based conjecture about the Pauline problem.

First, we note that there is a great deal of diversity between the Epistles. The distance, say, between Romans and 1 Thessalonians is greater than that between any two Gospels in respect of the same features. Hence, if the Epistles are all by the same author, that author displayed a great deal of versatility in respect of the quantifiable features we have been studying.

Secondly, we note that the Epistle to Titus stands at a great distance from every other Epistle except the Pastorals; and even from 2 Timothy it is as far as Acts is from the Pauline corpus. A correlation test of this kind is likely to exaggerate the dissimilarity

Table 14.23. *Verbs in the Pauline Corpus: Cross-tabulation of Mood by Tense*

	Present	Imperfect	Future	Aorist	Perfect	Pluperfect	Total
Indicative	1,433	84	318	751	247	1	2,834 (51.3%)
Subjunctive	173			318	5		496 (9.0%)
Optative	0		0	31	0		31 (0.6%)
Imperative	318			97	1		416 (7.5%)
Infinitive	284		0	226	19		529 (9.6%)
Participle	785		1	225	130		1,141 (20.7%)
Participle (Imperative)	63			6	5		74 (1.3%)
TOTAL	3,056 (55.4%)	84 (1.5%)	319 (5.8%)	1,654 (30.0%)	407 (7.4%)	1 (0.0%)	3,521 (100.0%)

Note

Blank cells represent forms which do not exist in Greek; cells marked zero represent possible forms which do not occur in the Pauline Corpus.

Source

Davison.

Table 14.24. Verbs in the Pauline Epistles: Moods other than the Indicative

Rom.	81 (6.9)	12 (1.0)	71 (6.1)	101 (8.6)
1 Cor.	152 (11.6)	3 (0.2)	104 (7.9)	101 (7.7)
2 Cor.	71 (9.3)	0	27 (3.5)	70 (9.2)
Gal.	33 (8.0)	3 (0.7)	24 (5.8)	32 (7.7)
Eph.	29 (8.9)	0	44 (13.5)	30 (9.2)
Phil.	19 (7.4)	0	26 (10.2)	39 (15.2)
Col.	23 (9.7)	0	34 (14.4)	11 (4.7)
1 Thess.	19 (7.8)	5 (2.1)	21 (8.6)	45 (18.5)
2 Thess.	16 (13.2)	4 (3.3)	9 (7.4)	19 (15.7)
1 Tim.	20 (6.7)	0	45 (15.1)	40 (13.4)
2 Tim	12 (5.3)	3 (1.3)	34 (15.0)	18 (8.0)
Titus	16 (14.0)	0	14 (12.3)	21 (18.4)
Philem.	5 (11.4)	1 (2.3)	4 (9.1)	3 (6.8)

Note

The figures in brackets after each frequency are the percentage of all verbs.

Source

Fribergs.

Table 14.25. Indicative Verbs: Distribution by Tense in the Epistles of the Pauline Corpus

Work	Present	Future	Imperfect	Aorist	Perfect	Total
Rom.	160 (46.8)	43 (12.6)	5 (1.5)	99 (28.9)	35 (10.2)	342
1 Cor.	234 (61.7)	43 (11.3)	6 (1.6)	59 (15.6)	37 (9.8)	379
2 Cor.	61 (44.5)	15 (10.9)	4 (2.9)	38 (27.7)	19 (13.9)	137
Gal.	48 (49.0)	11 (11.2)	7 (7.1)	21 (21.4)	11 (11.2)	98
Eph.	37 (50.7)	5 (6.8)	1 (1.4)	30 (41.1)	0	73
Phil.	7 (22.6)	9 (19.0)	2 (6.5)	12 (38.7)	1 (3.2)	31
Col.	28 (57.1)	3 (6.1)	2 (4.1)	11 (22.4)	5 (10.2)	49
1 Thess.	7 (31.8)	3 (13.6)	0	9 (40.9)	3 (13.6)	22
2 Thess.	12 (52.2)	6 (26.1)	0	4 (17.4)	1 (4.3)	23
1 Tim.	31 (52.5)	3 (5.1)	0	19 (40.4)	6 (10.2)	59
2 Tim.	14 (29.8)	11 (23.4)	0	19 (40.4)	3 (6.4)	47
Titus	8 (44.4)	0	0	8 (44.4)	2 (11.1)	18
Philem.	3 (50.0)	0	0	2 (33.3)	1 (16.7)	6
Paul	650 (50.6)	152 (11.8)	27 (2.1)	331 (25.8)	124 (9.7)	1,284

Note

Only verbs in the third-person singular are included.

Source

Fribergs.

*Table 14.26. Indicative Verbs: Distribution by Voice in the Epistles of the
Pauline Corpus*

Work	Active	Middle	Passive	Deponent
Rom.	215 (62.9)	7 (2.0)	72 (21.1)	48 (14.0)
1 Cor.	260 (68.6)	7 (1.8)	85 (22.4)	27 (7.1)
2 Cor.	95 (69.3)	5 (3.6)	19 (13.9)	18 (13.1)
Gal.	69 (70.4)	5 (5.1)	20 (20.4)	4 (4.1)
Eph.	57 (78.1)	5 (6.8)	9 (12.3)	2 (2.7)
Phil.	24 (77.4)	0	3 (9.7)	4 (12.9)
Col.	37 (75.5)	1 (2.0)	4 (8.2)	7 (14.3)
1 Thess.	15 (68.2)	3 (13.6)	1 (4.5)	3 (13.6)
2 Thess.	17 (73.9)	2 (8.7)	4 (17.4)	0
1 Tim.	38 (64.4)	1 (1.7)	12 (20.3)	8 (13.6)
2 Tim.	29 (61.7)	1 (2.1)	3 (6.4)	14 (29.8)
Titus	13 (72.2)	0	4 (22.2)	1 (5.6)
Philem.	3 (50.0)	0	2 (33.0)	1 (16.7)
Paul	872 (67.9)	37 (2.9)	238 (18.5)	137 (10.7)

Note
Only verbs in the third-person singular are included.

Source
Fribergs.

of a small text to much longer ones: but despite that, Philemon,
which is smaller than Titus, and 2 Thessalonians which is not
much longer, fit reasonably well into the corpus. Titus, therefore,
must be under suspicion.

We can take a rough measure of how well each Epistle is at home
in the Pauline corpus: we can sum the coefficients (though they are
not strictly additive). Those which fit snugly will have higher totals
than those which are at the edge. If we do this we get the following
ranking, from the most comfortable to the least: Romans, Philippians, 2 Timothy, 2 Corinthians, Galatians, 2 Thessalonians,
1 Thessalonians, Colossians, Ephesians, 1 Timothy, Philemon,
1 Corinthians, Titus. Romans and Philippians can therefore be
regarded as at the centre of the constellation. If we leave Titus out of
account, we find that the greatest distance is between Ephesians
and Colossians on the one hand, and 1 Corinthians on the other.

Various explanations may be given of the relationships revealed
by this table. One thing seems clear. There is no support given by

Table 14.27. *Correlations between Epistles in the Pauline Corpus in respect of Ninety-six Features*

	Rom.	1 Cor.	2 Cor.	Gal.	Eph.	Phil.	Col.	1 Thess.	2 Thess.	1 Tim.	2 Tim.	Titus
1 Cor.	0.9683											
2 Cor.	0.9810	0.9769										
Gal.	0.9821	0.9762	0.9785									
Eph.	0.9752	0.9144	0.9564	0.9404								
Phil.	0.9693	0.9510	0.9759	0.9632	0.9605							
Col.	0.9718	0.9198	0.9632	0.9435	0.9944	0.9698						
1 Thess.	0.9699	0.9540	0.9851	0.9679	0.9568	0.9727	0.9604					
2 Thess.	0.9787	0.9362	0.9683	0.9674	0.9691	0.9712	0.9709	0.9741				
1 Tim.	0.9395	0.9373	0.9439	0.9341	0.9179	0.9569	0.9316	0.9295	0.9248			
2 Tim.	0.9730	0.9447	0.9642	0.9604	0.9587	0.9781	0.9667	0.9531	0.9601	0.9771		
Titus	0.8738	0.8786	0.8726	0.8895	0.8540	0.9046	0.8876	0.8574	0.8590	0.9595	0.9325	
Philem.	0.9560	0.9193	0.9463	0.9560	0.9435	0.9611	0.9444	0.9459	0.9640	0.9231	0.9577	0.8659

this table to the idea that a single group of Epistles (say the four major Tübingen Epistles) stand out as uniquely comfortable with one another; or that a single group (such as the Pastoral Epistles) stand out as uniquely diverse from the surrounding context. 2 Timothy, one of the commonly rejected Pastoral Epistles, is as near the centre of the constellation as 2 Corinthians, which belongs to the group most widely accepted as authentic. It is only Titus which is shown as deserving the suspicion cast on the Pastorals.

What is to be said of the authorship of the Epistles is in the end a matter for the Scripture scholar, not the stylometrist. But on the basis of the evidence in this chapter for my part I see no reason to reject the hypothesis that twelve of the Pauline Epistles are the work of a single, unusually versatile author.

15

Sentence-length and Positional Stylometry

AMONG the ninety-nine indicators which were used in the studies in the previous chapters we did not include any statistics of sentence-length in the works considered. This may have surprised some readers, since it has been claimed that sentence-length distributions hold the key to a number of authorship attribution problems, in particular to the enigma of the Pauline Corpus. In the present chapter I will try to explain why I think the study of sentence-lengths, or of any feature which depends on punctuation, is of very ambiguous value in this context.

The serious study of sentence-lengths in Greek began with W. C. Wake's paper in the *Proceedings of the Royal Statistical Society* in 1957, 'Sentence-length Distributions of Greek Authors'. This paper showed that sentence-length distributions were not normal, but skew, and recommended their description by quantiles. It attempted to establish that the sentence-length distribution for a Greek author remained constant, within sampling error, throughout his work. Wake was aware that objection could be taken to the study of Greek sentence-length on the grounds that the punctuation of Greek text was not original, and in modern editions varies from editor to editor. Wake claimed, illustrating his point from two modern editions of Aristotle's *Categories*, that the differences between different editions were statistically insignificant.

A. Q. Morton, in *Paul, the Man and the Myth*, applied Wake's methods to the Pauline Epistles. But first he sought, by a study of a large number of Greek authors, to confirm Wake's hypothesis that the variation to be observed within the work of a single author was no greater than would be expected from random sampling of a homogeneous population. He worked out the mean, median, first quartile, third quartile, and ninth decile, with the appropriate standard errors, for the Epistles of Clement, samples from Clement of Alexandria and Philo, the histories of Herodotus and

Thucydides, the speeches of Lysias, Demosthenes, and Isocrates. Taking a distance of three standard errors from the population value of a constant as his measure of significant divergence in a sample, he concluded that in general there were no statistically significant differences within the work of a single author between samples of a reasonable size (100 sentences or more). There were, however, limits to this generalization: it did not hold for dialogue, or commentary, or texts preserved with lacunae. If these qualifications are respected, the hypothesis can be regarded as well-established. 'No exceptions have come to light except when the limits of the hypothesis were being established by deliberately applying it to extreme cases, such as dialogue, all of which lie outside the definition of continuous homogeneous prose.' Thus, if we take the first 200 sentences of each of the books of Herodotus and Thucydides, 'in no instance is there any difficulty in treating the parts of the work as samples drawn from the whole work; all the constants lie within the range of three standard errors'. Of those genuine works of Demosthenes long enough to test, only one falls outside the permissible range, and that is because it is quoting a law. Isocrates' works span a period of sixty-three years; one or two of his very late works show a discrepancy, which show that sentence-length distributions must be used with caution when the time covered by the samples is over fifty years (p. 63).

Again, following Wake, Morton turned to the study of the sentence-length distributions within the Pauline corpus. He took Galatians, Ephesians, Philippians, Colossians, 1 Thessalonians, 1 and 2 Timothy as samples in their entirety; Romans was divided into four samples, the first three samples of 150 consecutive sentences and the fourth of the remaining 131 sentences. 1 Corinthians provided four samples of 150 sentences (with an unsampled remainder of 28 sentences). 2 Corinthians was divided at the end of Chapter Nine: the first nine chapters provided two samples (100 and 108 sentences) and the third sample consisted of the 126 sentences starting from Chapter Ten. The constants of the sentence-length distributions are reproduced from *Paul, the Man and the Myth* in Table 15.1.

Morton sums up the evidence from this table as follows.

The examination of the constants of these distributions reveals the existence of a group, Group I, of four Epistles, Romans, I and II Corinthians, and Galatians, with anomalies in the first samples of both Romans and II Corinthians. Clearly separated from Group I, are the isolated Epistles to the Hebrews and to the Ephesians. Another group, Group 2, is made up of Philippians, Colossians, I and II Thessalonians. The Pastorals cannot be separated from this Group 2, and to it may belong part of the first sample of II Corinthians (p. 91).

Having gone on to examine the rates of occurrence of καί, δέ, ἐν, αὐτος and εἶναι in the Epistles, Morton draws his general conclusion:

In all tests Romans, I and II Corinthians and Galatians form a group. Within the group, differences are found in parts of Romans and II Corinthians, but these Epistles have been shown, by literary analysis, to have anomalies where the statistical evidence indicates them to be. Between the group and the other Epistles exist a large number of significant differences, some of these larger than any differences known to exist in the writings of any other author of Greek prose regardless of literary form or any other factor. It is not possible to explain these differences without assuming a difference of authorship (p. 94).

Twelve years later, in 1978, Morton returned to the topic in his book *Literary Detection*. He published a new set of constants for the sentence-length distributions. (These are based on a more recent edition of the New Testament, though this is not made clear to the reader, nor is the edition specified.) These are reproduced in Table 15.2. He also showed that the sentence-length distributions could be regarded as log-normal, and published the statistics of the distribution as measured on a log scale. Morton sets out the limits set, on a linear scale, by adding two standard errors to the statistics of Galatians. They are as follows:

	Mean	Median	First quartile	Third quartile	Ninth decile
Upper limit	15.32	12.27	7.95	18.05	28.66
Lower limit	12.24	9.47	5.86	13.41	17.62

He points out that statistically significant differences appear in the statistics of Ephesians, Colossians, 1 Thessalonians, and Hebrews

Table 15.1. *Sentence-length Distributions of the Pauline Corpus*

Epistle	Mean	Standard error	Median	Standard error	First quartile	Standard error	Third quartile	Standard error	Ninth decile	Standard error
Rom.										
1	14.6	0.98	9.5	0.67	5.38	0.58	20.6	1.26	28.3	3.06
2	12.3	0.73	9.3	0.59	5.72	0.51	16.3	1.26	23.2	1.67
3	10.8	0.62	8.5	0.49	5.44	0.43	13.6	1.02	19.7	1.15
4	12.1	0.72	9.8	0.53	6.74	0.46	13.7	0.60	19.1	1.56
TOTAL	12.30	0.39	9.2	0.28	5.82	0.24	14.9	0.46	23.4	0.86
1 Cor.										
1	11.9	0.69	9.6	0.64	5.7	0.55	14.9	0.78	21.4	2.6
2	10.0	0.56	8.2	0.41	5.6	0.36	11.9	0.95	16.9	1.4
3	11.0	0.61	9.2	0.56	5.8	0.48	13.4	0.63	19.5	3.7
4	10.5	0.52	8.6	0.49	5.6	0.43	13.5	0.92	19.4	1.2
TOTAL	10.8	0.29	8.7	0.25	5.6	0.21	13.4	0.39	19.1	0.63

2 Cor.										
1	13.5	0.9	13.8	1.0	8.5	1.1	21.0	1.5	27.2	1.7
2	13.1	0.9	10.7	1.2	6.4	0.7	19.1	2.0	23.7	1.4
3	12.7	0.8	8.6	0.6	5.3	0.5	15.2	1.5	22.4	2.4
TOTAL	13.1	0.5	10.6	0.7	6.3	0.4	17.9	0.8	24.6	0.9
Gal.	12.4	0.6	10.3	0.67	6.6	0.47	15.0	0.58	22.6	1.7
Eph.	24.3	2.07	17.5	1.8	11.3	0.9	31.7	3.6	47.5	7.5
Phil.	15.9	1.07	12.6	0.81	9.9	0.84	18.50	1.46	32.3	2.3
Col.	19.0	1.42	20.1	1.75	9.3	1.16	29.5	2.50	41.2	4.6
1 Thess.	18.1	1.34	14.0	1.32	8.53	0.85	22.6	2.17	34.1	2.3
1 Tim.	14.8	0.99	12.4	0.99	7.36	0.83	18.3	1.12	24.7	1.6
2 Tim.	14.0	1.12	11.9	1.03	6.0	1.20	17.4	1.28	28.5	4.7
Heb.										
1	18.2	0.92	14.2	0.68	10.1	0.63	21.3	0.88	34.2	1.5
2	14.3	0.72	11.6	0.75	7.6	0.55	17.4	1.4	26.4	1.7
TOTAL	15.9	0.63	12.7	0.50	8.2	0.44	19.4	0.95	30.5	1.9

Source

Morton and McLeman, *Paul, The Man and the Myth*.

Table 15.2. *Sentence-length Distributions of the Pauline Epistles which contain more than Fifty Sentences*

Epistle	Statistics and standard error of statistic									
	Mean	Standard error	Median	Standard error	First quartile	Standard error	Third quartile	Standard error	Ninth decile	Standard error
Rom.	14.33	0.50	10.55	0.55	6.45	0.30	18.32	0.93	27.21	2.39
1 Cor.	12.23	0.34	9.70	0.31	6.05	0.27	15.09	0.71	21.89	1.07
2 Cor.	15.99	0.71	13.01	0.94	7.02	0.51	21.25	1.15	29.66	1.30
Gal.	13.78	0.77	10.87	0.70	6.90	0.52	15.73	1.16	23.14	2.76
Eph.	30.31	3.21	19.00	2.22	10.50	0.81	37.00	3.87	58.75	3.33
Phil.	13.59	1.60	13.68	1.22	8.13	1.00	25.50	6.69	36.13	4.64
Col.	23.98	2.41	17.89	2.90	9.11	1.26	29.69	2.21	50.00	12.18
1 Thess.	22.77	2.06	18.18	1.85	9.67	1.17	31.25	2.93	46.67	4.06
1 Tim.	16.03	1.19	13.55	1.31	7.44	0.98	19.81	1.13	31.00	2.99
2 Tim.	16.05	1.52	12.61	1.00	7.02	1.46	19.38	3.79	32.00	13.17

Source
Morton, *Literary Detection*.

in the mean; Ephesians, 1 Thessalonians, and Hebrews for the median; and Ephesians and Hebrews for the first quartile, 2 Corinthians, Ephesians, Colossians, 1 Thessalonians, and Hebrews for the third quartile; Ephesians, 1 Thessalonians and Hebrews for the ninth decile. If we take a log scale, the log mean for Galatians is 1.025, with a standard error of 0.021. Statistically significant differences on the log scale, Morton tells us, appear between the means of Galatians and the means of Ephesians, Philippians, Colossians, 1 Thessalonians, and Hebrews. Here as in his earlier work, Morton takes it as axiomatic that Paul is, by definition, the author of the Epistle to the Galatians, and therefore is the author of all and only that part of the corpus which is homogeneous with Galatians.

There is no doubt that Wake and Morton have drawn attention to a very striking feature of the Pauline corpus. The variation in sentence-length between Galatians and Ephesians is quite enormous, and there is no way in which the two Epistles can be regarded as samples from a population homogeneous in this respect. The difficulties felt by scholars in the use of sentence-length, as an artificial construction from editorial punctuation, can be removed, Morton claims, if a sentence is defined as a group of words which end with a full stop, a colon, or an interrogation mark: for the main differences between editors lies in the use of the colon versus the period. The striking feature, Morton has claimed in a number of studies over the last two decades, is that the same single group of four major Epistles stands out from a great variety of independent tests–tests of sentence-length, of the occurrence of common words, and of the position of words and features in sentences. Unless there is some malign coincidence, this constant isolation of the four major Epistles is best explained on the hypothesis that they and they alone are the work of the Apostle Paul.

In fact, we have already seen in the previous chapter that a much more thorough study than Morton's of the most common words and grammatical features in the Pauline corpus does not at all isolate the four major Epistles as a single group. But even the argument drawn from sentence-length alone is flawed, as I shall now try to show.

In the first place, the discrepancies between the constants published in *Paul, the Man and the Myth* and in *Literary Detection* cast doubt on the thesis that the differences between sentence-lengths in different modern editions of a Greek text are statistically insignificant and can be disregarded. Compare, for instance, the distribution for Romans in the two works.

No. of words in sentence	1966	1978
1-5	110	78
6-10	214	160
11-15	113	101
16-20	57	52
21-25	42	51
26-30	15	14
31 +	30	42
TOTAL	581	498

Now it is true that if we take this distribution as a 7×2 contingency table and work out chi-squared, the value is only 10.73018 for six degrees of freedom, which is not significant at the 5% level. On the other hand, particular constants vary from edition to edition, and it is variation of this kind which has been used as an argument for rejecting common authorship. Thus the mean given for Romans in 1966 was 12.30, with a standard error of 0.39; the mean given in 1978 is 14.33 with a standard error of 0.50. The two means differ by more than twice the sums of the standard errors, and hence by the criterion used in *Literary Detection* they should come from works of different authors. The means for 1 Corinthians and 2 Corinthians likewise differ by more than twice the sums of the standard errors. It may be argued that the two-standard-error limit sets too strict a criterion for homogeneity, and that the appropriate limit is three standard errors, corresponding to a 0.003 level. But if we adopt this level and apply it to Morton's figures, then the differences from Galatians which he detected in other Epistles in the median and first quartile cease to be statistically significant. Indeed there seems to be an inconsistency in Morton's treatment, when the three-standard-error criterion is used to prove the consistency of works such as the histories of Herodotus and Thucydides, while the two-standard-error criterion is used to exclude all but the four major Epistles from being genuinely Pauline. However, it must be admitted that even using the three-standard-error criterion Ephesians and Colossians cannot be regarded as being homogeneous, in respect of sentence-lengths, with Galatians or Romans.

But there are discrepancies between the major Epistles, and between samples of the major Epistles, which are greater than those admitted by Morton. For the figures given in 1966, the mean of Romans is 12.30 and the standard error is 0.39. Two of the four samples of Romans have means outside the limits of three standard errors from the population mean. One sample of 1 Corinthians has a mean more than three standard errors from the Epistle mean of 10.8. In Romans, if we look at the ninth decile, we find that three out of four of the samples are distant by more than three standard errors from the population constant of 23.4. In the chart given in *Literary Detection*, the mean given for 1 Corinthians is distant from the mean given for 2 Corinthians more than thrice the sum of their standard errors. It is true that each of them could have come from the same population as Galatians, but they could not have come from the same population as each other.

Moreover, the alleged homogeneity of the works of other Greek writers, which is contrasted with the variation in the Pauline corpus, is itself overstated. This can be illustrated from the first Epistle of Clement. It is true that each of the samples here has a mean which is less than three standard errors from the means of the other samples; but where the samples are taken from a known population this is not the appropriate test for homogeneity. Morton gives us the mean for the population, the first Epistle, as 15.0 with a standard error of 0.4. Three of his four samples have a mean less than 13.8, and therefore more than three standard errors less than the population mean.

Despite all this, it cannot be denied that the Epistles of the Pauline corpus cannot be regarded as homogeneous in respect of sentence-length. To put it in the graphic terms illustrated in Chapter 4, there is no way of drawing a horizontal line through the bars on a graph marking the three standard error limits of the constants of the sentence-length distribution. But we need not conclude anything from this about authorship: many alternative hypotheses would explain the data, including an absurdly simple chronological one.

Suppose we assume that as he grew older, Paul grew fonder of longer sentences. (Something of the kind was remarked upon in Plato, in the article by Wake mentioned earlier.) Suppose further that we assume the following chronological order of the Epistles: Galatians, 1 Corinthians, Romans, 2 Corinthians, Philippians, 1 Thessalonians, 2 Thessalonians, Ephesians, Colossians. The data collected by Morton are then consistent with the hypothesis that Paul's sentences grew longer as he grew older. This can be represented graphically. Figure 15.1 shows the log-mean sentence-length of the Epistles listed in Morton's *Literary Detection*, with the margin of three standard errors on each side of the points marking the mean. It will be seen that a straight line can easily be drawn through all the bars on the chart: not a horizontal line,

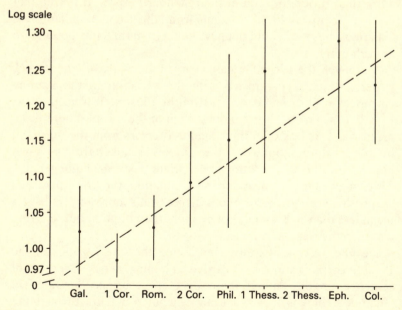

Fig. 15.1. Mean sentence-lengths of the Epistles.

which would indicate uniformity over time, but a sloping line corresponding to a correlation between sentence-length and increasing age.

Note that this represents the simplest possible form of the chronological hypothesis: it assumes that the gap in time between each pair of succeeding Epistles is uniform, and that the increased fondness for long sentences progresses in a uniform and linear manner. I am not putting forward the order of Epistles shown on the chart as a serious hypothesis about the actual order of writing. My purpose is merely to illustrate the kind of alternative hypothesis that is no less consistent with the data than variation in authorship. By relaxing the crude constraints that the Epistles must be equidistant on the time-scale, and that the increase in length must be linear, many different chronological hypotheses could be accommodated to the data presented by Morton.

In addition to studying the sentence-lengths and word frequencies in connection with the Pauline problem, Morton has also

Table 15.3. Conjunctions in Preferred Positions in the Pauline Corpus

Work	No. of sentences	K1	D2	G2	E1
Rom.	498	22	85	116	32
1 Cor.	555	28	122	74	42
2 Cor.	273	18	49	57	49
Gal.	166	3	46	28	14
Eph.	80	11	9	5	0
Phil.	86	8	15	8	3
Col.	66	8	1	5	4
1 Thess.	66	5	14	19	1
2 Thess.	35	3	10	6	0
1 Tim.	77	3	12	7	4

Note

K1 indicates a sentence with καί as its first word; D2 indicates a sentence with δέ as its second word; G2 indicates a sentence with γάρ as its second word; E1 indicates a sentence with εἰ as its first word.

Source

Morton, *Literary Detection*.

combined the two studies in a method which he calls positional stylometry. He has studied, for instance, not just the overall frequency of καί, but also the frequency of καί as the first word in a sentence; not just the overall frequency of δέ and γάϱ but the number of sentences which contain these conjunctions as their second word. Table 15.3 sets out his results, which are claimed to lend further support to the hypothesis that only the four first Epistles are genuinely Pauline.

Let us examine these data more closely to see how far they support this claim. We can divide the sentences in each Epistle into those which have καί as the first word, those which have εἰ as the first word, and those which have neither. Thus, for the first four Epistles, we get the following pattern:

	Sentences beginning with καί	No. beginning with εἰ	Others
Romans	22	32	444
1 Corinthians	28	42	485
2 Corinthians	18	49	206
Galatians	3	14	149

We can then take these Epistles in pairs, and see, by applying a chi-squared test to each of the 3 × 2 contingency tables, whether the difference between Epistle and Epistle are significant. We find that the differences between Romans and the other three Epistles are not significant at the 1% level (though Romans and Galatians differ at the 5% level). So too the difference between 1 Corinthians and Galatians is not significant. But the chi-squareds for 2 Corinthians/1 Corinthians (21.85) and betwen 2 Corinthians and Galatians (14.07) are highly significant.

Corresponding figures for the positional stylometry of δέ and γάϱ are set out in Table 15.4. Once again, the results are ambiguous. Undoubtedly Colossians and Ephesians (which do not differ significantly from each other) show a very different pattern from that of the four major Epistles. Chi-squared for Ephesians compared with Romans is 16.73 for two degrees of freedom, compared with 1 Corinthians 10.04, with 2 Corinthians 13.49, and with Galatians 17.24. But the major Epistles cannot themselves be

Table 15.4. Positional Stylometry for δέ and γάϱ

Epistle	Sentences with δέ as second word	Sentences with γάϱ as second word	Others
Rom.	85	116	297
1 Cor.	122	74	359
2 Cor.	49	57	167
Gal.	46	28	92
Eph.	9	5	66
Phil.	15	8	63
Col.	1	5	60
1 Thess.	14	19	33
2 Thess.	10	6	19
1 Tim.	12	7	58

Source
Derived from Table 15.3.

regarded as homogeneous. The difference between Romans and Galatians is significant (9.90), and is greater than that between Romans and Philippians, 1 Timothy, or either Thessalonians. Philippians fits well with both the major group and the Ephesians group.

Some years ago I made extensive studies of the occurrences of δέ and γάϱ as the second word of sentences in the Aristotelian corpus, taking samples from about a hundred works, genuine and suspect. I discovered that there was indeed a general similarity between the samples; but that to have used statistically significant differences as a rigid criterion for variation in authorship would have ruled out central works of undoubted Aristotelian provenance.*

Another positional study undertaken by Morton concerns the grammatical category of the last words of sentences. By studying the frequency of different categories (nouns, aorist verbs, non-aorist verbs, others) in the final position of a sentence, he claimed to provide a further independent test for discriminating between the writing of Greek authors. He presented his results in an article with S. Michaelson, 'Last Words: A Test of Authorship for Greek

* My results were presented in an article 'The Stylometric Study of the Aristotelian Writings', *CIRPHO Review*, Autumn 1975-6. The test would reject *Metaphysics Z* and *H*, and *Nicomachean Ethics* VI.

Writers', which was published in *New Testament Studies*, 18, 192-208. The conclusions of this article were severely criticized in a later article in the same journal by P. F. Johnson, 'The Use of Statistics in the Analysis of the Characteristics of Pauline Writing', 20, 92-100.

Michaelson and Morton had claimed that this test, too, showed that Galatians and 1 Corinthians in themselves and in combination formed a homogeneous sample, from which a 'Pauline expectation' could be derived; and that only Romans and 2 Corinthians presented observed results which accorded with this expectation. Johnson, while accepting that the variations in the Galatians and 1 Corinthians samples are such as could be expected to arise in random sampling about once in four times, criticizes the methodology of the 'Pauline expectation' which, he claims, neglects the fact that the 'expectations' are themselves variables, since they are derived from samples and not from the entire population of Pauline writing. A correct application of tests for association between sample passages, he claims, yields a picture quite different from that presented by Morton and Michaelson.

Table 15.5 sets out the frequencies of last words of different categories in the major Epistles, as recorded by Morton but corrected by Johnson to eliminate quotations and repetitions. Calculation of chi-square for the samples from each of the Epistles to the Corinthians shows them to be internally homogeneous. So too is Galatians, though only if we accept the 1% and not the 5% level of significance. But chi-squared for the seven Roman samples is 32.12 for twelve degrees of freedom, for which the probability is only 0.1%. The hypothesis that Galatians, and both Corinthian Epistles, could all be random samples from the same population has to be rejected: chi-squared for six degrees of freedom is 22.87, for which again the probability is only 1%. Once again, the claim that the four major Epistles form a uniquely homogeneous corpus within the Pauline writings is a claim that evaporates on close investigation. 1 Thessalonians, Philippians, 1 Timothy, and 2 Timothy all diverge less than Romans does from Michaelson and Morton's standard of Pauline last words.

Here again I have used the test proposed by Michaelson and

Table 15.5. Last Words of Sentences in Paul

Sample	Number of last words which are				
	Nouns	Aorist verbs	Non-aorist verbs	Others	Total
1 Cor					
1	30	7	22	13	72
2	22	7	32	20	81
3	22	8	37	12	79
4	24	8	33	12	77
5	28	6	33	11	78
6	25	8	29	15	77
7	14	3	11	13	41
TOTAL	165	47	197	96	505
Gal.					
1	36	9	22	9	76
2	21	10	24	21	76
TOTAL	57	19	46	30	153
2 Cor.					
1	9	2	3	6	20
2	29	4	18	19	70
3	3	0	1	3	7
4	13	4	11	17	45
5	32	7	68	77	248
TOTAL	86	17	68	77	248
Rom.					
1	7	2	3	8	20
2	36	4	24	4	68
3	32	15	13	18	78
4	25	5	18	22	70
5	22	14	15	13	64
6	28	3	30	13	74
7	10	1	3	8	22
TOTAL	160	44	106	86	396

Morton on all the works of the Aristotelian corpus. And once
again, while the majority of Aristotelian works did resemble one
another in respect of this feature, it was clear that to use the last-
word test as a criterion of authorship would lead to absurd
results.*

* The results are presented in an article cited above on p. 113. The test would
reject books IV and IX of the *Nicomachean Ethics*, and the second and third books of
the *Politics*.

16

Constraints and Prospects

MANY biblical scholars are hostile to, or at least suspicious of, stylometric methods. Twenty years ago Principal T. M. Knox wrote 'The spirit moveth where it listeth and is not to be reduced to the numerical terms with which alone a computer can cope.' To this day many would share his sentiments. Their resistance to stylometry may even have been reinforced by some of the exaggerated claims that have been made for it. It is no wonder when New Testament scholars resent being told that the computer has revolutionized scholarship, has brought science into Bible study, and has revealed for the first time the lineaments of what previous generations of students have ignorantly worshipped in their blindness.

Such claims are quite untrue and bring discredit upon the use of stylometric analysis in authorship attribution studies. It is wrong to suggest that each author has a stylistic fingerprint, and to compare the computer to a microscope which reveals fine details which remained hidden from the naked eye of the literary scholar. If we are to compare the stylometrist's procedure to a piece of scientific apparatus, the appropriate comparison is with the camera of an aerial photographer. Photography from the sky can enable patterns to be detected which are obscured when one is too close to the ground: it enables us to see the wood despite the trees. So the statistical study of a text can reveal broad patterns, macroscopic uniformities in a writer's work which escape notice as one reads word by word and sentence by sentence. These regularities are unobserved by the reader intent on content and style, though they might in fact be contributing considerably to the text's overall literary impact.

In the context of authorship attribution stylometric evidence should not be regarded as superseding or trumping external and internal evidence of a more traditional kind. The stylometrist simply brings his contribution of new evidence, of a less familiar kind, to be weighed in the balance along with the indicators to which we have been long accustomed. And indeed the kind of evidence provided by stylometry is not altogether new: for centuries scholars have studied vocabulary frequencies in the shape of *hapax legomena*, and stylists have taken pleasure in identifying authors' favourite constructions. The computer has provided better concordances to aid the study of quantifiable stylistic features, and the development of statistical techniques enables us to study variable features which are neither once-occurring nor monotonously regular. These innovations allow us to draw inferences from common words as well as rare words, and to allow for the variation to be expected even in a homogeneous corpus. Thus the new methods enable us sometimes to add to, and sometimes to discount, the evidence collected by traditional methods. But what the stylometrist is studying is essentially something that has always been studied since literary criticism began.

This comes out clearly enough in the writings of some of those who have been most critical of recent developments. Thus the late Professor Caird, discussing the authenticity of the Epistle to the Ephesians, allows that its style is not that of Romans. 'Its long sentences are loosely constructed with a profusion of purpose clauses, relatives and participles with a piling up of prepositional phrases, with strings of genitives, often with pairs of synonyms held together in seeming tautology. About all this there is no dispute.' But, Caird continues, it has been demonstrated that every stylistic feature of Ephesians can be paralleled in other Pauline letters: there are long sentences in Romans and Colossians; Romans can provide examples of the piling up of prepositional phrases to a degree unequalled in Ephesians, and there are strings of genitives in other Epistles. Therefore we cannot use these features as an argument against the authenticity of the Epistle.

Now it is clear that the features which Caird is discussing are quantifiable features: quantification merely gives precision to the vague words 'long', 'loose', 'profusion', 'piling up', 'strings', and so on. Moreover, the stylometrists are undoubtedly right in thinking that the correct way to study these quantifiable features is to examine the overall distribution in different letters, rather than to seek for isolated occurrences in one letter to parallel frequent features in another. This book contains a comparatively elementary attempt to study with precision the kinds of features listed by Caird as indicators of style.

If some other stylometric studies exasperate the reader by their arrogance, the present one may well have wearied him by its dullness. The information we have presented is in itself pedestrian, and the conclusions we have drawn have been extremely modest: that John's Gospel is very unlike the Apocalypse, that Luke and Acts are close enough to permit us to regard them as the work of the same author, and that the Pauline problem is not to be solved by regarding only the first four Epistles as the work of a single hand. Do we need all this elaborate study to produce such predictable conclusions?

In these last pages I do not wish to deny the very modest scope of the book. Indeed I wish to emphasize the limits, both of the stylometric method and of my own competence. But I wish also to explain why the cautious and provisional nature of the study may be a merit.

The most serious limitation of the statistical study of literary texts concerns the difficulty of applying stylometric methods to short passages. This affects the confidence of conclusions both about short works (such as the Epistle to Titus) or about short passages alleged to be interpolations (such as the final chapter of Romans). The difficulty is not merely the general difficulty, in statistical studies, of drawing conclusions about large populations from small samples: there is also a peculiar problem inherent in the literary subject-matter.

It is well understood that small samples may mislead about the characteristics of larger populations: that a particular hand at bridge, for instance, may contain many hearts and no spades, even though it has been fairly dealt from a normal pack. Statistical theory is well equipped to deal with this problem: the apparatus of standard errors, chi-squared tests, and the like enables us to discover how far it is rational for us to generalize from samples about the population from which they are drawn.

But in some subject-matters there is an additional difficulty presented by the periodicity of the phenomena being studied. If we wish to generalize about the climate of a country by studying its annual records over a period of ten years, we should have to allow for sampling variation if we were not to be misled in our conclusions. But if we were to try to generalize about a year's weather from the records of a single month we would have to take into account in addition the fact that weather comes in annual cycles. Similar caution is necessary in dealing with literary texts, since language is a periodic phenomena. To take a striking example suggested by A. Q. Morton: the frequency of 'and' in many texts is about one in twenty: but if we regard its occurrence as a random variable, we would expect to find 'and and' about once every 400 hundred words. The difficulty with language is greater than that with climate; for we know that the weather cycle is annual, but the periodicity of most literary phenomena is unknown, and will take many comparative studies to establish. All we can do is to study samples of sufficient length to feel reasonably secure that the periodicity can be discounted.

This is one reason why in the present work statistics have in general been given only for New Testament works as a whole; there has been no attempt to work on small samples within works, or to cut out from the calculations passages which scholars regard as interpolations. Before applying statistical tests to assist in the determination of hypotheses about interpolation, it is important to establish the characteristics of the text as a whole. To eliminate alleged interpolations to begin with, or to compare an allegedly interpolated portion of the text with an allegedly authentic one is to introduce subjectivity from the start into an objective test, and is to run the risk of *petitio principii*. The appropriate procedure is to ascertain the characteristics of the text as a whole, and then look for passages which reveal themselves as incongruous within it.

The statistics presented here represent the New Testament works as a whole, as they stand in the current Nestle edition, including even the quotations. It may be queried whether this is appropriate. On the one hand, it is of course a relevant feature of someone's style that he uses quotation at all: so a stylometric study should include among other things statistics about the frequency of quotation. On the other hand, it is clear that a quotation is not an unbiased sample of an author's own style, and so it should be left out of the database for any statistical study.

Probably the ideal solution is to give the statistics of quotations, and to omit quotations from the base for the statistics of the work as a whole. But it is not a simple matter to put this into practice. Only undoubted and verbatim quotes should be dealt with in this way. Only undoubted quotations should be excluded, because otherwise one is introducing the element of subjectivity that the statistics method is intended to check. Only verbatim quotes should be excluded, because the alteration of a quoted text may be a very vivid indicator of an author's style, showing how he adapts even other people's language to his own preferred pattern.

In the case of the New Testament this means in practice that it is only exact quotations from the Septuagint which come into question. Only in that case do we have undoubted sources, and control over the accuracy of the quotation. Though even there there is a problem: if we have a difference between Paul and our MSS of the Septuagint do we take that as a sign of Paul's adaptation, or as independent and perhaps preferable evidence for the Septuagint text?

In the present work the ideal solution has not been pursued, and the easier course taken of including quotations in the text. Table 16.1 shows the number of words in the Pauline Epistles which are quotations of the LXX text. This will give an indication of the extent to which quotations may or may not have distorted statistics. The test of quotation, for purposes of this table, has been the crude one of whether a passage appears in bold type in Nestle-Aland.

There are a number of New Testament problems which have not been touched on in the present work, but which may have light thrown upon them by the data collected here. Anyone interested, for instance, in the authenticity of the Johannine Epistles would not find it difficult to assemble, from our statistics for the fourth Gospel, a list of features which differentiate the evangelist from other New Testament writers. It would then be possible to look through the Epistles to see whether they bear these marks. Once again a warning is needed that no one should look for a Johannine fingerprint. There is no stylistic fingerprint: at most a signature–

Table 16.1. *Quotations in the*
Pauline Epistles

Epistle	Words from LXX
Rom.	654
1 Cor.	122
2 Cor.	83
Gal.	99
Eph.	59
Phil.	0
Col.	0
1 Thess.	0
2 Thess.	0
1 Tim.	4
2 Tim.	0
Titus.	0

for style, like a signature, can be voluntarily varied by an author, and impressively copied by a forger.

The most difficult of New Testament problems to submit to stylometric testing is the synoptic problem. Nothing has been said about it in this work. But the data presented about three synoptic Gospels may be of value to those who are interested in the problem: for the basis of any hypothesis about the interrelationship and prehistory of these Gospels must be a minute comparison of the existing texts of the completed works.

Again, I have expressed no opinion on the relationship of the Epistle to the Hebrews to the Apostle Paul. I have excluded it from the Pauline corpus simply on the grounds that it does not present itself as being Paul's in the way that the other Epistles do. I was in fact interested to note–as the reader no doubt will have done–the surprising number of features in which it resembles the Pauline corpus. Whether this is to be attributed to Pauline authorship or influence, or to something called 'epistolary genre', I express no opinion.

Not only has the present work held aloof from many interesting authorship attribution problems in the New Testament, it has also refrained from using any but the more elementary statistical techniques. Some of the problems studied, such as the Pauline canon, would be suitable for treatment by more advanced methods such as cluster analysis. I have made some experiments with such techniques, and my results do not suggest any answers different from those presented here. But I am insufficiently confident that I–or for that matter my most likely readers–understand such techniques adequately; hence I have not published the results of my investigations in this area. Though such analysis would not, I believe, be likely to alter any of the conclusions presented here, it would undoubtedly permit a more sophisticated and graphic method of presenting the evidence.

Overall, I have thought it best to present in simple and unvarnished form the data I have assembled, and to apply them only to some of the easier problems of New Testament scholarship. Those who are more learned in biblical studies, and more competent in statistical methods, will, I hope, be able themselves to make use of my data for more exciting purposes.

At least I hope to have shown that stylometry presents no threat to traditional biblical scholarship. The way forward lies in a combination of statistical and traditional methods; co-operation between the aerial photographer and the archaeologist on the ground, as it were. If the computer reveals that in certain passages there are more genitives and datives than expected, or that the proportion of articles to nouns is high, it is for the literary scholar to look and see what are the constructions which are producing these crude macroscopic effects. The ideal is to identify features which are frequent enough to provide the bones of a statistical analysis, and which yet have enough significant flesh for the philologist to feel that he is dealing with genuine stylistical choices of an author. The work presented in the present book is merely a preliminary study towards such an ideal. But it suggests to me that as the stylometrist's work progresses it will illumine a familiar landscape, rather than overturn beloved landmarks.

Appendix

The Ninety-nine Features used in the Final Test

1. Number of occurrences of καί
2. Number of occurrences of the verb εἶναι
3. Total number of conjunctions
4. Number of hyperordinating conjunctions (CH)
5. Number of co-ordinating conjunctions (CC)
6. Number of subordinating conjunctions (CS)
7. Number of occurrences of ἀλλά
8. Number of occurrences of δέ
9. Number of occurrences of γάρ
10. Number of occurrences of οὖν
11. Number of occurrences of ἐάν
12. Number of occurrences of εἰ
13. Number of occurrences of οὐ
14. Number of occurrences of μή
15. Number of occurrences of ἵνα
16. Number of occurrences of ὅπως or ὥστε
17. Number of occurrences of ὅτι
18. Number of occurrences of ὡς
19. Total number of particles
20. Number of sentential particles (QS)
21. Number of interrogative particles (QT)
22. Number of verbal particles (QV)
23. Total number of prepositions
24. Number of prepositions taking the accusative (PA)
25. Number of prepositions taking the genitive (PG)
26. Number of prepositions taking the dative (PD)
27. Number of occurrences of ἐν
28. Number of occurrences of εἰς
29. Number of occurrences of ἐκ
30. Number of occurrences of ἀπό
31. Number of occurrences of ἐπί
32. Number of occurrences of πρός
33. Number of occurrences of διά
34. Number of occurrences of κατά
35. Number of occurrences of μετά
36. Total number of articles
37. Number of articles in the nominative
38. Number of articles in the accusative
39. Number of articles in the genitive
40. Number of articles in the dative
41. Number of masculine articles
42. Number of feminine articles
43. Number of neuter articles
44. Number of articles in the singular
45. Number of articles in the plural
46. Total number of nouns
47. Number of nouns in the nominative
48. Number of nouns in the vocative
49. Number of nouns in the accusative
50. Number of nouns in the genitive
51. Number of nouns in the dative
52. Number of masculine nouns
53. Number of feminine nouns
54. Number of neuter nouns
55. Number of nouns in the singular
56. Number of nouns in the plural
57. Number of occurrences of θεός
58. Total number of third-person pronouns
59. Number of such pronouns in the nominative
60. Number of such pronouns in the accusative
61. Number of such pronouns in the genitive
62. Number of such pronouns in the dative
63. Number of masculine third-person pronouns

64. Number of feminine third-person pronouns
65. Number of neuter third-person pronouns
66. Number of third-person pronouns in the singular
67. Number of third-person pronouns in the plural
68. Number of occurrences of αὐτός
69. Total of adjectives (standard, pronominal, demonstrative, relative)
70. Number of standard adjectives
71. Number of pronominal adjectives
72. Number of demonstrative adjectives
73. Number of relative adjectives
74. Number of standard adjectives in the nominative
75. Number of such adjectives in the accusative
76. Number of such adjectives in the genitive
77. Number of such adjectives in the dative
78. Number of occurrences of πᾶς
79. Number of standard adverbs
80. Number of comparative adverbs
81. Number of relative adverbs
82. Number of interrogative adverbs
83. Total number of verbs
84. Number of verbs in the subjunctive
85. Number of verbs in the optative
86. Number of verbs in the imperative
87. Number of verbs in the infinitive
88. Number of verbs in the third-person singular indicative
89. Number of such verbs in the present tense
90. Number of such verbs in the future tense
91. Number of such verbs in the imperfect tense
92. Number of such verbs in the aorist tense
93. Number of such verbs in the perfect tense
94. Number of such verbs in the pluperfect tense
95. Number of such verbs in the active voice
96. Number of such verbs in the middle voice
97. Number of such verbs in the passive voice
98. Number of such verbs as are deponents
99. Occurrences of the verb λέγειν

These ninety-nine features are used in comparing the major sections of the New Testament. In comparing the Pauline Epistles, the same features are used with the following exceptions. The numbers of non-standard adverbs are not sufficient to justify dividing them into separate classes, and accordingly features 80, 81, and 82 are lumped together into a single category of non-standard adverbs. In the Pauline Epistles there are no occurrences of the pluperfect tense, and accordingly feature 94 is absent. The comparison between the Pauline Epistles is therefore based on ninety-six rather than ninety-nine different features.

Bibliography

Aland, K. *Vollständige Konkordanz zum griechischen NeuenTestament* (1975-83) I, 1975; II, *Spezialübersichten*, 1978.
— *et al.*, *The Greek New Testament*, 3rd edn., 1966.
Bachmann, H. and Slaby W. A. *Computer-Konkordanz zum Novum Testamentum Graece*, 1980.
Davison, M. E. 'Computer Analysis of Verb Forms in the Greek New Testament', *ALLC Bulletin*, 11 (1983), 68-73.
— 'Paul v. Luke: A Computer Analysis of Some Differences', *ALLC Bulletin*, 12 (1984), 1-4.
Friberg, B. and T., *Analytical Greek New Testament*, 1981.
— 'A Computer-assisted Analysis of the Greek NT Text', in Patten, D. and Holoien, R. (eds.) *Computing in the Humanities* 1-49.
Fuchs, W. *Nach allen Regeln der Kunst*, 1968.
Grayston, K. and Herdan, G., 'The Authorship of the Pastorals in the Light of Statistical Linguistics', *New Testament Studies* 6 (1960), 1-15.
Harrison, P. N. *The Problem of Pastoral Epistles*, 1921.
— *Paulines and Pastorals*, 1964.
Johnson, P. F. 'The Use of Statistics in the Analysis of the Characteristics of Pauline Writings', *New Testament Studies*, 20 (1974), 92-100.
Kenny, A., 'The Stylometric Study of the Aristotelian Writings', *CIRPHO Review*, Autumn 1975-6.
Maredsous, Abbey of, *Informatique et Bible*, 1982.
Michaelson, S. and Morton A. Q., 'Last Words: A Test of Authorship for Greek Writers', *New Testament Studies*, 18 (1972), 192-208.
Morgenthaler, R., *Statistik des neutestamentlichen Wortschatzes*, Zurich, 1958; *Beiheft ur 3. Auflage*, 1982.
Morton, A. Q. *Literary Detection*, 1978.
— and McLeman J. J., *Paul, the Man and the Myth*, 1966.
—, Michaelson, S., and Thompson J. D. *The Computer Bible*, 1980- .
Neirynck, F., 'La Nouvelle Concordance du Nouveau Testament', *Ephemerides Theologicae Lovanienses*, 54 (1978), 323 ff.
Wake, W. C. 'Sentence-length Distribution of Greek Authors', *Proceedings of the Royal Statistical Society*, 1957.

Index